Classics

SUSSEX

COUNTY CRICKET CLUB

John Barclay, Sussex CCC captain 1981-86 and currently director of cricket and coaching at the Arundel Castle Cricket Foundation.

JOHN WALLACE

Sussex CCC – first Gillette Trophy winners in 1963, from left to right, back row: G.C. Cooper, R.J. Langridge, D.L. Bates, A. Buss, J.A. Snow, L.J. Lenham. Front row: N.I. Thomson, J.M. Parks, E.R. Dexter (captain), A.S.M. Oakman, K.G. Suttle.

First published 2003

Tempus Publishing Limited
The Mill, Brimscombe Port,
Stroud, Gloucestershire, GL5 2QG

British Library Cataloguing in Publication Data.
A catalogue record for this book is available from the British Library.

ISBN 0 7524 2739 3

Typesetting and origination by Tempus Publishing Limited
Printed in Great Britain by Midway Colour Print, Wiltshire

Foreword

Set between 1827 and 2002, these charming little episodes beautifully depict the greatest moments of the club. They are served up and presented as tasty morsels which whet the appetite for more to come. As I read each lovely piece, I found myself feverishly flicking over the pages as the writer described one player after another performing great feats. The end product is as much a potted history of Sussex Cricket as a commentary upon dramatic matches.

I have learnt a lot too. How many readers will know about the deadly effect of Walter Humphreys' lobs in the 1880s? How intriguing that this outmoded style should totally bamboozle the Australians at Hove and reduce them to gibbering wrecks in defeat. Perhaps the subtle brand of bowling should be resurrected and set to challenge the current Australians in all their pomp. Humphreys was still going strong in 1893 when W.G. Grace twice failed for Gloucestershire, who were soundly beaten, and the mighty Humphreys was carried shoulder-high back to the pavilion.

Few would argue that no two players in Sussex's history had a greater or more dominant influence upon the game than Ranjitsinhji and Fry at the turn of the century. It seems almost inconceivable now that Sussex failed in that time to win the County Championship. How interesting it was to read that Yorkshire, great rivals at the time, resorted to bowling wide of Fry's off-stump to restrict his scoring. They were not successful and Sussex's golden age continued to flourish.

How I rejoiced to read that, during an encounter with Somerset at Taunton in 1919, the ball was constantly being fished out of the River Tone. In 1985 I was on the receiving end myself when the mighty Vivian Richards took a liking to my off-spin and deposited three balls in one over into the river. What an honour it is now to be included in this book having played a part in Sussex's great victory over Somerset in 1978.

There are so many fine Sussex names and matches to savour here, which will bring back happy memories for everyone. Which is the greatest of all these matches, I wonder, and whose is the most memorable performance? There are so many famous players and occasions to choose from. Enjoy some (mostly) glorious Sussex days as you savour the past and make your choice.

John Barclay
Sussex CCC Captain 1981-1986
Director of Cricket and Coaching,
Arundel Castle Cricket Foundation

Acknowledgements

I am most grateful indeed to John Barclay, Director of Cricket at the Arundel Castle Foundation, for writing a foreword, and to James Howarth, Kate Wiseman and Becky Gadd at Tempus Publishing for their constant help and guidance. For the loan of the majority of the original scorecards and numerous photographs, I am deeply indebted to Nicholas Sharp who has so readily made them available to me from his outstanding collection.

I am, as ever, in the debt of Rob Boddie, honorary librarian at Sussex County Cricket Club, for the loan of photographs and other material and for his ready encouragement and support. I also owe much to Roger Packham, who has kindly read the text with great care and made a host of valuable amendments.

In addition, I should like to thank John Fowling, Francesca Watson, Peter Wynne-Thomas, Tony Laughton (for the Albert Craig quotations), the staff of the Brighton Local Studies Library and *The Cricketer* magazine for their willing help. For the use of photographs, I acknowledge Angela Moore and Lindsay Vass (especially for the cover photo), the *Brighton Argus* (for the photograph of Jason Lewry which appears on p.124), Bill Smith, Roger Ockenden and George Herringshaw (*www.sporting-heroes.net*) and others whose photographs may have been used inadvertently without acknowledgement.

Bibliography

Wisden Cricketers' Almanack (relevant editions)
The Cricketer (relevant editions)
The Playfair Cricket Annual (relevant editions)
Sussex County Cricket Club Handbook (relevant editions)
John Marshall, *Sussex Cricket* (Heinemann, 1959)
John Barclay, *The Appeal of the Championship* (Fairfield Books, 2002)
Benny Green, *Wisden Anthology 1864-1982* (Queen Anne Press, 1979)
Benny Green, *The Wisden Book of Cricketers' Lives* (Macdonald Queen Anne Press, 1986)
Christopher Martin-Jenkins, *World Cricketers* (Oxford University Press, 1996)
Simon Heffer (ed.), *The Daily Telegraph Century of County Cricket* (Sidgwick and Jackson, 1990)
Andrew Ward, *Cricket's Strangest Matches* (Robson Books, 1999)
Bob Jones and Nicholas Sharp, *Sussex Cricket Postcards (1901 to 1947)* (County Print Services, 1994)
David Green, *The History of Gloucestershire County Cricket Club* (Christopher Helm, 1990)
George Washer, *A Complete Record of Sussex County Cricket 1728 to 1957* (1958)
C.B. Fry (ed.), *The Book of Cricket* (George Newnes, 1900)
C.W. Alcock (ed.), *Famous Cricketers and Cricket Grounds* (Hudson and Kearns, 1895)
P.C. Standing, *Cricket of Today* (Blackwood, Le Bas and Co., 1900)
The Brighton Herald
The Daily Telegraph
Sussex Daily News

Alan Wells, Sussex CCC captain 1992-1996 and the County's outstanding batsman in the 1990s.

Classic Matches

1827	*v.* England	Darnall	Friendly
1855	*v.* Yorkshire	Sheffield	Friendly
1886	*v.* Lancashire	Hove	County Championship
1888	*v.* Australians	Hove	Tourist Match
1888	*v.* Kent	Tonbridge	County Championship
1893	*v.* Gloucestershire	Hove	County Championship
1899	*v.* Kent	Tonbridge	County Championship
1899	*v.* Australians	Hove	Tourist Match
1902	*v.* Essex	Leyton	County Championship
1902	*v.* Surrey	Hastings	County Championship
1903	*v.* Yorkshire	Bradford	County Championship
1906	*v.* Middlesex	Hove	County Championship
1907	*v.* Kent	Canterbury	County Championship
1911	*v.* Nottinghamshire	Hove	County Championship
1913	*v.* Lancashire	Horsham	County Championship
1919	*v.* Somerset	Taunton	County Championship
1922	*v.* Hampshire	Southampton	County Championship
1924	*v.* Middlesex	Lord's	County Championship
1926	*v.* Warwickshire	Horsham	County Championship
1929	*v.* Kent	Hastings	County Championship
1930	*v.* Northamptonshire	Hove	County Championship
1933	*v.* Middlesex	Hove	County Championship
1936	*v.* Nottinghamshire	Hove	County Championship
1938	*v.* Australians	Hove	Tourist Match
1939	*v.* Derbyshire	Derby	County Championship
1939	*v.* Yorkshire	Hove	County Championship
1947	*v.* Glamorgan	Hove	County Championship
1951	*v.* Kent	Tunbridge Wells	County Championship
1953	*v.* Leicestershire	Leicester	County Championship
1957	*v.* Gloucestershire	Hove	County Championship
1960	*v.* Middlesex	Hove	County Championship
1963	*v.* Worcestershire	Lord's	Gillette Final
1964	*v.* Warwickshire	Worthing	County Championship
1966	*v.* Leicestershire	Leicester	County Championship
1972	*v.* Australians	Hove	Tourist Match
1972	*v.* Surrey	Eastbourne	County Championship
1978	*v.* Somerset	Lord's	Gillette Final
1981	*v.* Derbyshire	Eastbourne	County Championship
1986	*v.* Lancashire	Lord's	NatWest Final
1987	*v.* Hampshire	Horsham	Sunday League
1991	*v.* Yorkshire	Middlesbrough	County Championship
1991	*v.* Kent	Hove	County Championship
1993	*v.* Glamorgan	Hove	NatWest Trophy
1993	*v.* Essex	Hove	County Championship
1993	*v.* Warwickshire	Lord's	NatWest Final
1996	*v.* Durham	Hove	County Championship

1997	*v.* Derbyshire	Derby	NatWest Trophy
1999	*v.* Gloucestershire	Hove	County Championship
2001	*v.* Hampshire	Hove	County Championship
2002	*v.* Somerset	Taunton	County Championship

Introduction

Cricket has been played in Sussex since time immemorial, well before the establishment of the County Cricket Club in 1839, and the selection of a mere fifty matches from the hosts of games that have taken place in the County presents the author with myriad problems. I have included one match from 1827 and another from 1855, but the remainder are Championship, tourist or limited-over games. I have included at least one match against every first-class county and, whenever possible, an original scorecard even though the writing may be a little indistinct in places and, occasionally, without bowling analysis.

One may perhaps be forgiven for pondering how to view the word 'classic'. The *New Oxford Dictionary* definition gives 'of the highest quality and outstanding of its kind' and I have taken that to mean a match where a tense finish came about or a great victory was achieved, or one in which players of either side particularly distinguished themselves, or even one perhaps where some unusual event occurred. I am sure it is possible to think of further definitions.

I am grateful to have received suggestions from friends in Sussex about the choice of matches and, having listened carefully, I have made some adjustments. Readers will doubtless wonder why a particular match has not found favour and, while I wish to sympathise with them, fifty is always going to be a small number in this context. I am anxious, however, to record that the final choice was mine.

I saw my first Sussex match in 1946, when a pupil at Collyer's School, Horsham, the *alma mater* of both George Cox junior and Paul Parker. My classmates and I were given the afternoon off – one doubts, sadly, the likelihood of such a thing occurring nowadays – to view the County taking on Glamorgan on the town's most attractive ground. Sussex collapsed to 35 all out in their first knock and lost by an innings and, although they finished last in the Championship that year, my enthusiasm was not dimmed. Following and supporting Sussex over a long period has, at times, been an uphill task, but if one embraces the idea of community with the county where one was brought up, nothing will ever shake it. Do I have a particular favourite match? Everyone does, and I am sure that mine must be the September day in 1963 when, still a mere Associate Member of MCC, I sat in the Warner Stand at Lord's and saw Sussex take the first one-day title. It was not an especially pleasant day, but the cricket had an intensity that I had not experienced before and, when Sussex won and Ted Dexter raised the Gillette Cup aloft, I knew that my faith in Sussex had not been misplaced.

Fifty matches, therefore, is a small number for a club that has existed for 163 years (and has played as a county for even more) and I now look forward perhaps to the possibility of finding and writing about another fifty that may help assuage the disappointment of those whose favourite match has not been included.

John Wallace,
January 2003

SUSSEX *v.* ENGLAND

4, 5 and 6 June 1827 — Friendly
New Ground, Darnall, Sheffield, Hallamshire

The edition of the *Sheffield Mercury* which appeared on 2 June 1827 contained an announcement in which Mr W.H. Woolhouse 'respectfully informed his friends and the public that the first match of a series of three between the players of Sussex and the best of All-England would commence on Whit Monday, 4 June 1827, on the New Ground at Darnall.' The notice went on to say that the match would begin precisely at 11.00 a.m. and that stumps would be drawn at 6.30 p.m. The Grand Stand had now been completed and presented 'every accommodation for select parties', while tents had been erected on the right-hand side of the ground from which an excellent view of the game was to be had. Gentlemen's tickets to the Stand would cost 2s 6d, while accompanying ladies would pay 1s each. Admission to the tents cost 1s and to the ground 6d.

The advertisement of the match in the *Sheffield Mercury* obviously reached far and wide because, as the match report noted, 'it caused a great number of visitors from all parts of the country to be present' on the Whit Monday, although poor weather on the Tuesday and the fact that the holidays were over on the Wednesday led to a gate that was less than expected on those days. Nevertheless, the report was lavish in its praise for the arrangements made by Mr Woolhouse and spoke of the excellent and reasonably-priced refreshments and the ample number of waiters who would fetch what was required 'without any tax upon you for their services'.

The teams appeared rather later than the advertised 11.00 a.m. as William Lillywhite and James Broadbridge opened the bowling and in the first nine balls dismissed three batsmen. Two more batsmen were out with 'but 2 notches got'. At 2 runs for 5 wickets, the England side looked in serious trouble, but Dawson and Fuller Pilch of Norfolk, 'a powerful young fellow, possessed of muscle and great activity', pulled the innings round so that England were finally all out 'with 81 notches got'. When the Sussex side went in, Lillywhite opened the batting with William Slater and, by the close, Sussex had lost 9 wickets for 78, with Dale and Meads, each on 22, still there.

Owing to overnight rain, the match was not resumed until 2.00 p.m. on the Tuesday. Dale and Meads continued their partnership and added a further 13 notches to give Sussex a lead of 10, a handy figure in a low-scoring match. England fared rather better in their second innings and batted through the remaining two hours' play. On the Wednesday morning, Marsden, Jupp, Pilch and Saunders batted well and took their side's total to 112. Brown was dismissed early in the Sussex second innings, 'but subsequently', to quote the match report, 'it was found there was no chance and the game was dropped' or, in other words, Sussex won by 7 wickets.

Darnall, near Sheffield.

THREE GRAND
CRICKET MATCHES,
For 1000 *Sovereigns.*

The First Match of the Three, between the Players of Sussex and the best of All England, commenced Playing on the New Ground, Darnall, on Whit-Monday Tuesday, and Wednesday, June 4th 5th, & 6th, 1827.

ALL ENGLAND.

First Innings.		*Second Innings.*	
1 — Flavell	0 bowled by Lillywhite	1 G. E. Dawson	15 bow. by J. Broadbridge
2 — Bowyer	0 hit wicket	2 — Jarvis	17 bowled by do.
3 J. Saunders	0 caught by Slater	3 W. Barber	1 do. by do.
4 W. Barber	1 caught by Dale	4 — Flavell	3 caught by Lillywhite
5 T. Marsden	0 hit wicket	5 F. Pilch	13 caught by Brown
6 G. E. Dawson	13 run out	6 — Jupp	20 caught by Lillywhite
7 F. Pilch	38 bowled by Lillywhite	7 T. Marsden	22 caught by Meads
8 — Matthews	2 ditto by ditto	8 J. Saunders	11 bow. by J. Broadbridge
9 — Beagley	17 ditto by ditto	9 — Beagley.	5 not out
10 — Jarvis	9 c. by J. Broadbridge.	10 — Bowyer	0 bow. by J. Broadbridge
11 — Jupp	0 not out	11 — Matthews	1 bow. by Lillywhite
Byes 1	Total 81	Byes 4	Total 112

SUSSEX.

First Innings.		*Second Innings.*	
1 W. Slater	0 caught by Pilch	1 G. Brown	1 caught by Marsden
2 W. Lillywhite	14 stumped by Saunders	2 G. Meads	21 bowled by Pilch
3 Wm. Broadbridge	14 caught by Pilch	3 T. Pierpoint	23 bowled by Marsden
4 J. Twaites	0 caught by Jarvis	4 J. Twaites	37 not out
5 Jas. Broadbridge	0 stumped by Saunders	5 Jas. Broadbridge	15 not out
6 T. Pierpoint	3 caught by Marsden		
7 G. Brown	2 bowled by Matthews	Byes 6	Total 103
8 J. Dale	31 not out		
9 C. Duff.	0 caught by Marsden	Sussex won with 7 wickets to go down	
10 C. Pierpoint	1 bowled by Flavell		
11 G. Meads	26 bowled by Matthews.		
	Total 91		

Umpire for Sussex, Mr, C. ROOTS, of Brighton.—Umpire for All England, Mr. JOSEPH DENNIS, of Nottingham.

NAMES OF THE GENTLEMEN BACKERS:—

H. TAMPLIN, Esq. on the part of Sussex; J. JENNER, Esq. on the part of All England.

☞ *Every attention will be paid to render the Returns as correct as possible.*

T. ORTON, PRINTER, HIGH-STREET, SHEFFIELD.

SUSSEX *v.* YORKSHIRE

27, 28 and 29 August 1855 Friendly
Bramall Lane, Sheffield

On 24 August 1855, *The Morning's News*, Sheffield announced that, on the following Monday, 27 August, a match between the players of Yorkshire and Sussex would take place on the ground of the United Club, near St Mary's Church in Sheffield. The match duly began on the Monday morning on the United Club's new ground at Bramall Lane. An unnamed Sussex player described it as follows: 'It is one of the finest grounds in England and has every convenience suitable for both players and public. It is enclosed by a ten-foot wall and there are beautiful stands and refreshment rooms for visitors.' As this Yorkshire-Sussex clash was seen as the first important match to be played there, it clearly excited great interest. John Wisden and James Dean opened the batting for Sussex to the bowling of Hodgson and Iddison. Wickets fell at regular intervals throughout the day, but Wisden, 'whose batting afforded a great treat to the lovers of the game', as the reporter for *The Morning's News* recorded it, was not to be dislodged despite constant bowling changes and, when play ended shortly after 6.00 p.m., he was still at the wicket with 138 to his name – the second century of his career – which eclipsed his score of exactly 100 made on the Higher Common Ground versus Kent at Tunbridge Wells in July 1850. Sussex's score stood at 246 for 6 wickets with the amateur Edwin Napper, from Wisborough Green, still partnering Wisden with 23 to his name.

The match continued on the Tuesday morning, and Wisden and Napper moved the Sussex score on to 260 before the former was caught at square-leg for 148, the only first-class century scored in the 1855 season. Sussex's tail wagged profitably and eventually a score of 292 was reached. The Yorkshire team were obviously not daunted by the impressive Sussex total, and Ellison and Chatterton scored a rapid 37 for the first wicket before the latter was dismissed. The second wicket did not go down until the score had reached 55 when John Lillywhite bowled Ellison, but subsequently the home side's wickets tumbled and Yorkshire found themselves dismissed for 103 and, 189 runs behind, they were required to follow-on. Their second innings was even less successful than their first, and they collapsed to 29 for 6 wickets against the bowling of Dean and the Lillywhite brothers. Then John Berry, batting at number three, and Ellison, coming in lower down the order, held firm so that, at the close, Yorkshire had reached 43 without further loss.

James Dean.

What appears to be have been a wholly unequal contest did not last for much longer on the Wednesday morning. The County's bowlers, aided by some smart fielding which yielded two run-outs, soon polished off the Yorkshire innings which ended on 72, leaving Sussex the winners by an innings and 117 runs. In the two innings, Dean bowled 214 balls and conceded 89 runs for his 8 wickets, while John Lillywhite, bowling two balls fewer than his partner, took 5 wickets for a mere 51 runs.

COUNTY OF SUSSEX v. COUNTY OF YORK.

This great County Match commenced playing at Sheffield, on Monday, August 27th, 1855, and was concluded on Wednesday, the 29th, when, as will be seen by the under score, Sussex beat their opponents in one innings by no fewer than 117 runs.

SUSSEX.

FIRST INNINGS.

J. Wisden, c Anderson, b Hodgson	**148**
Dean, b Hodgson	13
Mr. W. Napper, l b w, b Crossland	7
John Lillywhite, c Iddison, b Wright	14
Box, c Anderson, b Wright	13
Wells, c Kaye, b Chatterton	8
Mr. E. Tredcroft, b Chatterton	21
Mr. E. Napper, c Hodgson, b Crossland	31
R. Payne, c Hodgson, b Wright	14
G. Brown, b Crossland	10
James Lillywhite, not out	2
Byes, 7; wide, 4	11
	292

YORKSHIRE.

FIRST INNINGS.		SECOND INNINGS.	
Mr. M. J. Ellison, b John Lillywhite	22	c Wisden, b John Lillywhite	6
G. Chatterton, c Wells, b Dean	21	not out	5
John Berry, c Wisden, b Dean	12	c Dean, b James Lillywhite	24
A. Crossland, c W. Napper, b Dean	21	b Wisden	7
H. Wright, c Wisden, b John Lillywhite	0	b Dean	0
G. Anderson, b Dean	3	c Brown, b John Lillywhite	5
W. Kaye, run out	9	c E. Napper, b John Lillywhite	0
H. Sampson, c Box, b Dean	2	run out	9
Mr. E. Kay, run out	0	run out	5
R. Iddison, c and b Dean	8	c James Lillywhite, b Dean	2
Hodgson, not out	3	b John Lillywhite	7
Byes	2	Leg byes	2
	103		72

COHEN, PRINTER, BRIGHTON.

Sussex v. Lancashire

9, 10 and 11 August 1886
Hove

County Championship

Sussex were able to field a stronger side for this match than the one which had played Lancashire earlier in the season. The amateurs Billy Newham, George Brann, Aubrey Smith and Freeman Thomas (later Lord Willingdon and Viceroy of India) were all available for this match and George Cotterill, the nephew of Dr Joseph M. Cotterill, was given his first game for Sussex.

Lancashire, having won the toss on the Monday morning, decided to take first use of the excellent Hove wicket. A.N. Hornby and Dick Barlow put on 51 for the first wicket, and a hard-hitting half-century by Robinson brought their total to 211 at quarter past four. Although the Hide brothers shouldered most of the bowling, Walter Humphreys' lobs accounted for the last four Lancashire batsmen at a cost of 26 runs. The hosts had just over one-and-a-half hours' batting on the first day and, although Jesse Hide and George Cotterill went cheaply and Billy Newham succumbed before the close, the County were handily placed at 98 for 3 wickets at 6.00 p.m. William Tester was well set on 39 and Freeman Thomas, missed before he had scored, was there at the close with 17 to his name.

The two overnight batsmen continued their stand on the Tuesday morning before both were out on the same score of 58, each having hit 7 boundaries. For all that, Sussex found themselves 11 runs adrift of their visitors' total. Rain had interrupted play during the morning and had certainly made the wicket a good deal less easy to bat on. Jesse Hide and Tester used the difficult wicket to their advantage and, with Humphreys chipping in again with 2 late-order wickets in 6 balls, Lancashire were bundled out for 60 in just ninety minutes. This left the County a mere 72 runs for victory.

On the Wednesday morning, the County made heavy weather of reaching their target, finally reaching a total of 73 in 71 overs. The redoubtable England all-rounder Barlow, who had collared 6 Sussex wickets for 54 in their first innings, was again on form and, aided by Watson's and Briggs' highly economical bowling, they reduced their opponents at one stage to 48 for 6, despite a typically resilient innings by Billy Newham. Jesse Hide and George Brann were, however, able to take root and, by just after one o'clock on the Wednesday afternoon, a flurry of boundaries by Hide had secured a win for Sussex.

Jesse Hide saw Sussex home.

Dick Barlow, a fearsome Lancashire all-rounder.

2d  2d

Sussex County Cricket Ground.

OFFICIAL SCORE

1886

Monday Tuesday, and Wednesday, August 9, 10, 11, between

SUSSEX and LANCASHIRE.

LANCASHIRE	First Innings	Second Innings
Mr. A. N. Hornby	c Smith b Tester ... 37	c Lucas b Tester ... 7
Barlow	c Phillips b J. Hide ... 30	run out ... 1
Mr. P. Dobell	c Phillips b Tester ... 0	run out ... 8
Briggs	c Newham b Tester ... 8	l-b-w b J. Hide ... 3
Mr. T Eccles	c Phillips b A. Hide ... 34	b Tester ... 1
Robinson	c J. Hide b A. Hide ... 54	c Tester b J. Hide ... 0
Mr. O. P. Lancashire	b Humphreys ... 24	c Smith b Tester ... 21
Yates	not out ... 15	c Cotterill b J. Hide ... 1
Mr. A. Teggin	st Phillips b Humphreys ... 0	c Tester b Humphreys ... 9
Watson	c Lucas b Humphreyr ... 9	c Lucas b Humphreys ... 6
Pilling	l-b-w b Humphreys ... 0	not out ... 2
	b. l.-b. w. n.-b. Total...	b. l-b. 1 w. n.-b. Total... 1
	Total .. 211	Total... 60

SUSSEX	First Innings	Second Innings
Tester	c Watson b Briggs ... 58	b Barlow ... 8
J. Hide	c Pilling b Barlow ... 4	not out ... 21
Mr. G. H. Cotterill	b Barlow ... 0	b Briggs ... 1
Mr. W. Newham	l-b-w b Watson ... 37	c Pilling b Barlow ... 25
Mr. F. Thomas	run out ... 58	b Watson ... 0
Mr. F. M. Lucas	c Pilling b Barlow ... 23	c Hornby b Watson ... 4
Mr. G. Brann	l-b-w b Barlow ... 3	not uot ... 8
W. Humphreys	not out ... 11	b Barlow ... 4
Mr. C. A. Smith	c Pilling b Barlow ... 0	
H. Phillips	b Barlow ... 0	
A. Hide	b Briggs ... 1	
	b. 2 l-b. 3 w. n.-b. Total... 5	b. 1 l.-b. 6 w. n.-b. Total... 7
	Total.. 200	Total... 73

Umpires ..Street and Pullen   Scorers... Messrs. Bates and Slatter

GRAND CRICKET WEEK. Aug. 23-4-5 Sussex v. Yorkshire, Aug. 26-7-8, Sussex v. Australians.

CROWHURST,
PRINTER TO THE S.C.C.C.
52, MARKET STREET, BRIGHTON.

Sussex v. Australians

19, 20 and 21 July 1888 — Tourist Match
Hove

Arthur Hide – awarded a silver cup for his bowling.

In 1884 Sussex had come close to defeating the Australians. Four years later, a side captained by Aubrey Smith and including five of the previous team, again did battle with the 'Colonials', as the local press liked to dub the visitors.

Sussex, on winning the toss, decided to bat. The decision seemed popular with the crowd, but when Walter Quaife, Francis Gresson and Jesse Hide were all quickly dismissed it looked as though the 'twin terrors', Charles Turner and Jack Ferris, were going to run through the County side. Billy Newham, however, was not so easily intimidated and, assisted by Freeman Thomas and George Brann, he brought the Sussex total to two short of the hundred, his own innings being described by the *Sussex Daily News* as 'deserving of the highest praise and forming an important feature in the succession of events leading to the ultimate victory'.

For all that, 98 was not a great score and, as the Australians applauded Newham back to the pavilion, they must have been thinking that the seeds of another routine victory had been sown. They were quickly disabused when Arthur Hide bowled Alick Bannerman with the first ball of their innings. The Sussex spectators became highly excited as the Australian wickets started to tumble and, when Walter Humphreys was brought on, his lobs proved too much for the middle and lower order and, in just ninety minutes, the powerful Australians had been dismissed for 68. This was too much for the crowd who, jumping over the ropes, made their way to the professionals' box and constantly cheered Arthur Hide (4 for 21) and Humphreys (5 for 21).

Sussex went in again and, closing on 74 for 3, must have been content with their day's work. Overnight, there was heavy rain and the Sussex batsmen had to do some 'gardening' as the wicket wore quite quickly. The hundred went up after half an hour, but the tail failed to wag and the innings closed, disappointingly, on 116. The Australians needed only 147 to win, albeit the highest total of the game.

Arthur Hide struck early by bowling Australian skipper Percy McDonnell and, although Bannerman and Harry Trott started to score quickly, the introduction of Humphreys brought a flurry of wickets so that, when rain brought an end to play, 6 wickets were down for 35 runs. Turner and Trott resumed on the damp Saturday morning and played so well that an Australian victory was not quite out of the question. The Sussex bowlers, however, stuck to their task. When the overnight pair had been dismissed, the rest of the innings collapsed and Sussex ran out easy winners by 58 runs, Arthur Hide (4-23) and Humphreys (4-19) again doing the most damage. The Sussex Committee were delighted and added a sovereign to each professional's customary fee, while a silver cup donated by Mr G. Munster was presented to Arthur Hide on account of his 8 wickets and 5 catches.

Albert Craig, well known for his ditties on Sussex cricket, was moved to compose 'British Grit Triumphant':

'Then here's to our cracks,
To the men of renown
Who without chance or luck
Took Australia down.
I'll warble their praises
Wheresoever I rove,
And wish them success
In each contest at Hove.'

ONE PENNY ONE PENNY

SUSSEX COUNTY CRICKET GROUND.

OFFICIAL SCORE, 1888.

Thursday, Friday, and Saturday, July 19, 20, and 21,
SUSSEX versus AUSTRALIANS

SUSSEX	First Innings	Second Innings
...Quaife	b Turner ... 0	c Jarvis b Ferris ... 26
...Mr. F. H. Gresson	b Turner ... 2	c Trott b Ferris ... 30
...Mr. W. Newham	not out ... 44	b Worrall ... 10
...J. Hide	b Turner ... 1	b Ferris ... 12
...Mr. F. Thomas	c Turner b Trott ... 13	c Worrall b Turner ... 14
...W Humphreys	c Bannerman b Trott ... 0	b Turner ... 13
...Mr. C. A. Smith (captain)	b Turner ... 6	st Jarvis b Ferris ... 2
...Mr. G. Brann	st Jarvis b Worrall ... 18	b Turner ... 9
...A. Hide	c Bonnor b Turner ... 4	b Turner ... 0
...H. Phillips	c Ferris b Trott ... 0	not out ... 0
...Tate	c Bonnor b Trott ... 2	b Turner ... 0
	b.8 l.-b w. n.-b. Total .. 8	b l.-b.w. n.-b. Total...
	Total ... 98	Total .. 116

1-1 2-6 3-8 4-37 5-37 6-48 7-78 8-94 9-94 10-98

1-49 2-66 3-66 4-90 5-92 6-105 7-109 8-109 9-116 10-116

AUSTRALIANS	First Innings	Second Innings
...Mr. A. C. Bannerman	b A. Hide ... 0	b Humphreys ... 9
...Mr. P. S. McDonnell	c A. Hide b J. Hide ... 3	b A. Hide ... 0
.. Mr. H. Trott	st Phillips b Humphreys ... 24	c Smith b A. Hide ... 25
...Mr. G. J. Bonnor	b A. Hide ... 2	b Humphreys ... 0
...Mr. J. McBlackham	l-b-w b Humphreys ... 17	c A. Hide b Smith ... 0
...Mr. A. H. Jarvis	b Humphreys ... 13	c A. Hide b Humphreys ... 1
...Mr. C. T. B. Turner	c Phillips b A. Hide ... 0	b A. Hide ... 39
...Mr. J. D. Edwards	c Humphreys b A. Hide ... 0	c Thomas b A. Hide ... 2
...Mr. J. J. Ferris	c A. Hide b Humphreys ... 6	not out ... 8
...Mr. J. Worrall	c A. Hide b Humphreys ... 0	b Humphreys ... 0
...Mr. J. J. Lyons	not out ... 3	b J. Hide ... 0
	b. l-b. w. n.-b. Total...	b. l.-b.4 w. n.-b. Total .. 4
	Total .. 68	Total ... 88

1-0 2-6 3-9 4-40 5-56 6-56 7-57 8-64 9-65 10-68

1-1 2-20 3-20 4-21 5-22 6-24 7-67 8-68 9-81 10-88

Umpires...Henty and Farrands Scorers...Stubberfield and Salter.

TELEGRAPH OFFICE ON THE GROUND.

SUSSEX *v.* KENT

2 and 3 August 1888 County Championship
Tonbridge

The fascinating uncertainty of a cricket match can rarely have been better seen than in Sussex's match with Kent at the Angel Ground in Tonbridge. Prior to the match, rain had fallen almost incessantly for a day and a half, and it was feared that the opening day would be washed out altogether. The Thursday morning, however, was bright and sunny and, as there was a drying wind, it was possible to start play just before four.

Aubrey Smith won the toss and decided to take first innings, but Sussex were soon in trouble on a wicket that was clearly unpredictable. The young amateur Francis Gresson struck a rapid 22, but the remainder of the Sussex batting collapsed before the bowling of 'Nutty' Martin and Walter Wright, the last 5 wickets falling for 8 runs. Kent were left with about an hour's batting and they, too, experienced difficulty with the pitch. Thus 3 wickets went quickly for the addition of only 4 runs and, at the close on the Thursday evening, the hosts were struggling at 33 for 5 wickets.

Friday morning dawned brightly, but the pitch had lost little of its spiteful nature. Although wickets fell consistently, mainly to the accurate bowling of Jesse and Arthur Hide, the ninth-wicket pair put on 43 runs together, which looked almost certain to win the match for Kent. When Sussex went in again with a deficit of 52 runs, the roller had temporarily calmed the wicket. When the openers easily put on 34, it looked as though Sussex might well take hold of the match. The bowling of Alec Hearne and Martin, however, was too good for the rest of the Sussex side, and even Billy Newham and George Brann were unable to turn the tide.

Fred Tate produced a remarkable display.

The County did better in their second knock, but they had left Kent a small total of 45 to win the match. The pitch at this stage was becoming increasingly difficult, but with such a small total to reach Kent did not look in any particular difficulty. They reached 41 for the loss of 4 wickets, so that they needed a further 4 runs with six 6 wickets left – a mere formality perhaps. At this point, Aubrey Smith decided to bring on Fred Tate, then in his second season for the County. The result, however, was electrifying: Tate, with his slow-medium off-spinners, immediately bowled George Hearne, who had batted patiently for 7 runs, and then castled four more batsmen in quick succession without conceding a run. When Martin came in to join Kemp, 2 runs were still needed, and 2 quickly-run singles, each of which might have resulted in a run-out, brought Kent home by a single wicket. Martin, with 10 wickets in the match and the scorer of the last 2 precious runs, was certainly Kent's hero, but Fred Tate's remarkable piece of bowling, allied to two catches off Arthur Hide's bowling, was the start of an outstanding career for Sussex in which he took over 1,300 wickets.

Sussex won the toss and elected to bat

SUSSEX				
Mr F.H. Gresson	c Wilson b Wright	22	b A. Hearne	18
W.Quaife	c Marchant b Martin	4	b Martin	10
Mr G. Brann	c and b Martin	0	c Wilson b A. Hearne	10
Mr W. Newham	b Wright	0	b A. Hearne	9
Mr J.M. Cotterill	c Wright b Martin	5	c G. Hearne b A. Hearne	3
J. Hide	b Wright	3	b Martin	1
W. Humphreys	b Martin	5	b A. Hearne	11
*Mr C.A. Smith	b Wright	1	c Fox b Martin	8
A. Hide	c Marchant b Martin	2	b A. Hearne	7
F.W. Tate	not out	0	c G. Hearne b Martin	7
#H. Phillips	st Kemp b Martin	1	not out	0
Extras	(b6, lb2)	8	(b9, lb3)	12
TOTAL		51		96

Bowling	O	M	R	W	O	M	R	W
Martin	24.2	11	27	6	35	20	23	4
Wright	24	15	16	4	6	0	14	0
A. Hearne					29.2	11	47	6

KENT				
Mr W. Rashleigh	b J. Hide	0	c Newham b A. Hide	12
Mr J.N. Tonge	c A. Hide b J. Hide	0	c Humphreys b A. Hide	2
Mr W.H. Patterson	b. J. Hide	4	c Tate b A. Hide	7
Mr C.J.M. Fox	c A. Hide b J. Hide	10	b Tate	11
Mr L. Wilson	lbw b A. Hide	12	c Tate b A. Hide	0
G.G. Hearne	lbw b J. Hide	1	b Tate	7
*Mr F. Marchant	b A . Hide	13	b Tate	0
W. Wright	not out	8	b Tate	1
#Mr M.C. Kemp	run out	7	not out	0
A. Hearne	b. A. Hide	28	b Tate	0
F. Martin	b J. Hide	10	not out	2
Extras	(b9, lb1)	10	(b3)	3
TOTAL		103	(for 9 wkts)	45

Bowling	O	M	R	W	O	M	R	W
A. Hide	42	24	46	3	26	14	21	4
J. Hide	37.2	21	33	6	22	14	20	0
Mr Smith	7	5	5	0				
Tate	13	7	9	0	4	3	1	5

Umpires: Jupp and Panter

Kent won by 1 wicket

Sussex *v.* Gloucestershire

22, 23 and 24 May 1893 County Championship
Hove

The weather was excellent when Sussex won the toss and decided to bat on an excellent wicket in front of a large home crowd. Sadly, the County's batsmen made only moderate use of their chances and reached a rather meagre 202 by mid-afternoon. Aubrey Smith and Billy Newham, who between them made 104 of the 192 runs from the bat, were the only players to distinguish themselves. Newham's innings was compact and cautious, but Smith struck 12 fours in a brilliant, if not wholly faultless, display. The end of the Sussex innings left Gloucestershire an hour and fifty minutes' batting and, although 3 wickets (including Dr W.G. Grace, who was caught off Fred Tate) fell for 52 runs, they ended the day without further loss on 133.

On the second morning, the two overnight batsmen – the Australian Jack Ferris and Sidney Kitkat – helped the visitors to build a significant lead. Ferris ran to his maiden hundred in first-class cricket and was seventh out at 243 after hitting 15 fours. Sussex went in again with a deficit of 95 runs and immediately the two Georges – the professional Bean and the Australian amateur Wilson – provided the large crowd with an immaculate display of batting. After a mere two hours and twenty minutes, they had scored 217 for the first wicket. When Wilson, who had struck 19 fours in his 105, was dismissed, Bean was just ahead of him on 107*. As another wicket fell at the same score, Sussex ended the day on 217 for 2 wickets, a handy lead of 122.

George Wilson, an Australian amateur.

The Hove wicket was showing little sign of wear and Sussex might well have felt themselves to be in the driving seat. But this pleasant anticipation was not realised, and William Murch and Fred Roberts bowled so well that the last 8 wickets fell for only 77 runs. Bean, the mainstay of the innings, was seventh out with the score on 254 after having hit 19 fours. The pendulum had now swung back to the visitors. Set only 200 to win, Gloucestershire and the 'Champion', Dr W.G. Grace, seemed to have a reasonably easy task on a wicket that was still playing well. Although Sussex enjoyed the encouragement of having dismissed both W.G. and Octavius Radcliffe (promoted to open with the great man) for only 23 runs, Ferris and John Painter raised the total to 127 in a partnership of 104 in only sixty-five minutes.

This stand appeared to have won the match for the visitors, but then another change came about. Billy Murdoch, the Sussex captain, decided to give Walter Humphreys and his lobs a turn. He came on with the score at 114 and, in the course of 5 overs, he dismissed 4 batsmen for 11 runs. 127 for 2 was soon transformed into 148 for 6 and the spectators, now realising that the home side were in with a chance, renewed

1d. **1d**

SUSSEX COUNTY CRICKET GROUND

OFFICIAL SCORE, 1893.

Whit-Monday, Tuesday & Wednesday, May 22 23 & 24.

SUSSEX v. GLOUCESTERSHIRE

SUSSEX	First Innings		Second Innings	
1 Bean	c Rice b Murch	12	c Board b Murch (~~not out~~)	120 (~~107~~)
2 Mr. G. L. Wilson	c Rice b Murch	18	c E. M. Grace b Robert	105
3 Mr. W. L. Murdoch (Cap)	b Ferris	18	c WG Grace b Roberts	9
4 Mr. W. Newham	c E. M. Grace b Roberts	34	not out	24
5 Mr. G. Brann	b Ferris	11	b Murch	5
6 Mr. C. A. Smith	c Painter b Murch	70	c Murch b Roberts	0
7 Guttridge	st Board b W. G. Grace	13	c De Winton b Murch	6
8 Humphreys	c Board b Murch	11	c Murch b Roberts	4
9 Tate	lbw b W. G. Grace	0	c De Winton b Roberts	0
10 Butt	not out	0	b WG Grace	12
11 Hilton	c Painter b Murch	5	LBW b WG Grace	4
	b5 l.-b.5 w. n.-b. Total	10	b.5 l-b. w. n.-b. Total	5
	Total	202	Total	~~217~~ 294

1-29 2-31 3-55 4-75 5-132 6-152 7-181 8-194 9-194 10-202

1-217 2-217 3-227 4-232 5-233 6-240 7-254 8-254 9-290 10-294

GLOUCESTERSHIRE	First Innings		Second Innings	
1 Mr. W. G. Grace	c Guttridge b Tate	17	b Tate	16
2 Mr. J. J. Ferris	c Tate b Guttridge	106	st Butt b Humphreys	47
3 Painter	c Smith b Hilton	4	b Humphreys	51
4 Mr. R. W. Rice	lbw b Humphreys	22	b Humphreys	2
5 Mr. S. A. P. Kitcat	st Butt b Smith	52	ct b Humphreys	14
6 Mr. O. G. Radcliffe	c Butt b Smith	0	c Bean b Tate	7
7 Mr. E. M. Grace	lbw b Humphreys	16	b Humphreys	26
8 Mr. S. De Winton	b Humphreys	22	st Butt b Humphreys	15
9 Murch	not out	38	st Butt b Humphreys	5
10 Roberts	b Tate	7	not out	2
11 Board	c and b Tate	4	b Smith	3
	b.4 l-b5 w. n.-b. Total	9	b.7 l.-b.1 w. n.-b. Total	8
	Total	297	Total	196

1-21 2-28 3-61 4-184 5-184 6 223 7-243 8-247 9-291 10-297

1-12 2-23 3-127 4-128 5-131 6-148 7-183 8-190 9-193 10-196

Umpires...Clements and Goodyear Scorers .. J. R. Bates and J. J. Smith.

Thursday, Friday and Saturday May 25, 26 and 27. SUSSEX v. SOMERSET.

Crowhurst, Printer, 52 Market Street, Brighton.

George Bean – opened well with Wilson.

Walter Humphreys, who was decisive in the County's success.

their interest. Edward Grace and George de Winton batted sensibly in a partnership of 35 before the latter was stumped. When Humphreys bowled Grace, only 10 runs were needed, but Murch was stumped after the addition of a further 3 runs and, with another 3 added, John Board was bowled by Aubrey Smith. Sussex had won an intriguing game of fluctuating fortunes by the narrow margin of 3 runs. Humphreys, whose 7 wickets for 30 runs in 17 overs were decisive in the County's success, was carried shoulder-high back to the pavilion. Albert Craig was, once more, wholly effusive about Sussex's success:

'With pleasure the heart of each Sussex man throbs
To see Walter Humphreys come off with his "lobs".
The conflict was keen, but the Sussex lads won it,
It isn't the first time good Humphreys has done it.'

SUSSEX *v.* KENT

5, 6 and 7 June 1899 County Championship
Kent

On some occasions Sussex have squandered an advantage in a match to the dismay of their supporters, but their match with Kent at Tonbridge in 1899 was one occasion when a losing situation was transformed into an excellent win. It also recorded the first time that a Sussex bowler took 10 wickets in an innings – a feat that has been achieved on only one subsequent occasion.

On the Monday morning, Kent won the toss and elected to bat. After an early loss of 2 wickets, Cuthbert Burnup and William Patterson dealt so firmly with the Sussex attack that a large score seemed in prospect. When Ernest Killick came on to bowl, however, and dismissed them both, a change came over the match. Despite some big hitting by 'Nutty' Martin, Kent's total was not as large as might perhaps have been expected. The Sussex innings began badly when George Brann was caught at the wicket off the first ball of the innings and the day ended with the County on 36 for 2 wickets.

On the Tuesday morning, wickets continued to fall steadily and, although Ranjitsinhji batted well, Sussex succumbed to the Kent bowlers and were invited to follow-on, as they were more than 120 runs behind. Although Brann again failed, Charles Fry and Ranjitsinhji came together with the score on 8 for 1 wicket and added 107 before the latter was dismissed, while Fry went on to bat for nearly three hours. Although skipper Billy Murdoch went quickly, another useful partnership formed between Killick and Billy Newham, which took Sussex through to 192 for 4 wickets at the end of the second day.

Killick was soon dismissed on the Wednesday morning and defeat again loomed, but Newham continued to bat well and, joined by Arthur Collins, he took Sussex to a position of safety. When they were finally all out, three hours' play remained and a draw seemed likely. But Kent had not reckoned on Cyril Bland at his fastest. In his first 3 overs, he conceded 13 runs, but in the next 7 overs, he took 6 wickets at a cost of only one more run. Although Alec Hearne stood fast and eventually took out his bat, 3 wickets were down for 21 and half the side were out for 25. Martin and Fred Huish helped Hearne stem the tide for a while, but when Bland was brought back, he quickly took the last 3 wickets and Sussex were home by 112 runs. Not only had Bland set a County record by taking all 10 wickets, but Harry Butt, often standing up behind the stumps, even to Bland, secured 8 victims, something which only William Broadbridge in 1826 and Harry Phillips in 1872 had bettered at the time. This satisfying win for Sussex certainly illustrated the view that asking one's opponents to follow-on may not always be the right course if the team batting again score heavily and gain a pyschological advantage.

Cyril Bland – first with all ten wickets for Sussex.

Harry Butt did well behind the stumps.

Kent won the toss and elected to bat

KENT

*Mr J.R. Mason	run out	1	c Butt b Bland	12
A. Hearne	c Murdoch b Tate	23	not out	55
Mr C.J. Burnup	c Brann b Killick	80	b Bland	1
Mr W.H. Patterson	c Butt b Killick	67	c Butt b Bland	0
Mr H.C. Stewart	c Butt b Bland	8	b Bland	0
Rev. W. Rashleigh	c Butt b Killick	0	c Butt b Bland	0
Mr G.J.V. Weigall	c and b Killick	29	c Butt b Bland	0
F. Martin	c and b Killick	42	b Bland	15
S. Brown	b Bland	1	b Bland	0
#F.H. Huish	not out	12	lbw b Bland	28
Mr W.M. Bradley	c Collins b Killick	1	b Bland	0
Extras	(b12, lb 1, w1)	14	(b 1, nb 2)	3
TOTAL		278		114

Bowling	O	M	R	W	0	M	R	W
Tate	33	13	70	1	16	9	21	0
Bland	31	5	81	2	25.2	0	48	10
Cox	17	7	28	0	3	1	10	0
Killick	20	7	44	6	10	0	26	0
Ranjitsinhji	15	4	28	0	4	1	6	0
Collins	5	0	13	0				

SUSSEX

Mr G. Brann	c Huish b Bradley	0	b Bradley	1
*Mr W.L. Murdoch	b Bradley	26	b Bradley	0
Mr A. Collins	c Huish b Hearne	5	not out	55
G. Cox	b Bradley	5	b Brown	15
Mr C.B. Fry	b Bradley	16	c and b Bradley	85
K.S. Ranjitsinhji	b Mason	43	c Hearne b Bradley	46
E. H. Killick	b Hearne	19	c Huish b Bradley	26
Mr W. Newham	c and b Mason	22	c Huish b Mason	61
#H.R. Butt	b Mason	3	lbw b Bradley	9
F.W. Tate	not out	8	b Bradley	19
C.H.G. Bland	b Mason	4	b Bradley	12
Extras	(b2, lb 1)	3	(b 11, lb 9, nb 1)	21
TOTAL		154		350

Bowling	O	M	R	W	O	M	R	W
Bradley	21	8	58	4	54.2	22	122	8
Hearne	17	8	22	2	37	17	54	0
Mason	16.1	8	35	4	38	14	73	1
Martin	10	5	15	0	27	8	46	0
Brown	6	1	21	0	12	3	34	1

Umpires: T. Mycroft and W. Clarke

Sussex won by 112 runs

Sussex *v.* Australians

27, 28 and 29 July 1899 Tourist Match
Hove

A visit by the Australians to Hove has always been popular and probably no more so than in 1899 when their side commanded just as much respect as it does nowadays. The opening Thursday morning was as if made for cricket: a warm sun shining in a blue sky and just sufficient breeze from the sea to keep the air fresh. It was estimated that a crowd of some 7,000 was packed into the ground and there was not a spare seat to be had in the members' pavilion and the covered stand. The occupants of the two ladies' tents displayed the latest fashions, while other members of the fair sex in white dresses and with dainty sunshades were content to sit on the hard benches or on the grass close to the boundary. The scene was set for a feast of cricket, and so it proved.

Ranjitsinhji won the toss for Sussex and, on a firm and well-prepared wicket, Charles Fry and George Brann opened against, in the words of the *Brighton Herald* correspondent, 'the terrible Ernest Jones, with deliveries that go whizzing past the head like a cannon shot, and the clever Monty Noble.' For all that, the Sussex pair posted the fifty in half an hour, and the score had reached 96 before Brann was bowled. Next in was Ranji, and the crowd, who obviously expected great things from him, were hugely disappointed when he quickly lost his off-stump just before lunch. After the interval Fry, now joined by Ernest Killick, set about the Australian attack and monopolised the scoring to such an extent that, when he reached his hundred after no more than two hours' batting, the total was only 145. Killick, having survived a chance to the 'keeper, then started to score as quickly as his illustrious partner and the County were in the fortunate position of having reached 300 with only 2 wickets down.

Fry, having gone past Alec Hearne's 168 for W.G. Grace's XI made a few days previously – the then highest score against the tourists – cast caution to the winds and was finally caught at slip, having batted for four hours. He hit 25 fours with scintillating drives and deft square- and late-cuts, and added 209 in partnership with Killick. After the latter had been dismissed, and Francis Marlow had scored 20 from 5

Victor Trumper, peerless Australian batsman.

Francis Marlow helped to save the game.

Australians won the toss and elected to bat

SUSSEX				
Mr C.B. Fry	c Trumble b McLeod	181	c and b Jones	10
Mr G. Brann	b McLeod	24	b Jones	0
*K.S. Ranjitsinhji	b McLeod	5	c Darling b Jones	15
E.H. Killick	b McLeod	106	b Hill	57
F.W. Marlow	c Trumper b Trumble	34	not out	20
Mr A. Collins	not out	35	not out	31
J. Vine	b Trumble	4		
F. Parris	c Noble b Jones	9		
F.W. Tate	c Trumble b McLeod	1		
#H.R. Butt	c Kelly b Trumble	5		
C.H.G. Bland	c Laver b Trumble	0		
Extras	(lb 10)	10	(b 6, lb 4)	10
TOTAL		414	(for 4 wkts.)	143

Bowling	O	M	R	W	O	M	R	W
Jones	44	9	147	1	17	4	30	3
Noble	21	9	31	0	3	1	11	0
Trumble	32.4	6	75	4	18	7	53	0
McLeod	48	20	91	5	6	3	7	0
Laver	5	0	26	0	1	1	0	0
Worrall	4	1	15	0				
Gregory	4	1	19	0				
Hill					5	0	16	1
Kelly					3	0	16	0

AUSTRALIANS		
H. Trumble	b Bland	26
J. Worrall	c Brann b Killick	128
V.T. Trumper	not out	300
S.E. Gregory	st Butt b Killick	73
C. Hill	c Butt b Brann	28
*J. Darling	not out	56
Extras	(b9, nb 4)	13
TOTAL	(for 4 wkts dec.)	624

M.A. Noble, F. Laver, #J.J. Kelly, C.E. McLeod, E. Jones did not bat

Bowling	O	M	R	W
Tate	35	6	113	0
Bland	38	4	170	1
Parris	23	6	69	0
Ranjitsinhji	8	1	29	0
Killick	28	6	80	2
Brann	29	5	70	1
Vine	14	3	52	0
Collins	8	2	28	0

Umpires:

V.A. Titchmarsh and W. Hearn

Match Drawn

Arthur Collins played his part in securing a draw.

The lunchtime crowd at Hove.

balls, including 3 successive fours off Jones, a few wickets went down, but the County must have been well satisfied with 389 for 6 wickets at the close. A collection made from the crowd for Killick raised £51 – about half-a-sovereign per run!

The Friday dawned as bright as the previous day and, again under a cloudless sky, the Australians soon polished off the Sussex tail. Jones, for all his pace, had singularly unflattering figures, while the more measured attack of Hugh Trumble and Charles McLeod paid greater dividends. When it was their turn to bat, the Australians at first showed some respect for the Sussex attack, and Trumble and Jack Worrall went slowly to 62 before the first wicket fell. This brought in the twenty-one-year-old Victor Trumper, the youngest member of the Australian team, and he and Worrall then began to take the County's bowlers apart. The score advanced to 240 before Worrall was caught at slip, having hit 22 fours and a mere 12 singles in a particularly hard-hitting innings. From then on it was all Trumper, as he hit four after four off the wilting County attack. By the close he had reached 175, and the Australian total stood at 388 for 2 wickets.

The Australian innings continued on the Saturday morning in much the same vein as on the previous evening. Nothing could stop Trumper and when Joe Darling closed the Australian innings with only 4 wickets down, Trumper had been at the wicket for six hours and twenty minutes. His 300 was not only the highest score of the visitors' tour, but also beat the 286* scored by the recently retired Sussex captain, Billy Murdoch, when he was playing for the Australian side in 1882 on the same ground. Trumper's innings was the first triple hundred recorded by an Australian tourist in England and only the second made by any batsman from Down Under.

On the Saturday afternoon, with two hours left for play, an Australian victory seemed on the cards when Fry, Brann and Ranji were all dismissed cheaply, but Killick added a half-century to his first innings ton, and Marlow and Arthur Collins batted out time to close, in a rather tame manner, a match which had otherwise produced some exhilarating cricket.

Sussex *v.* Essex

30 June, 1 and 2 July 1902 County Championship
Leyton

Billy Newham, then in his forty-second year, had not wanted to play against Essex in the 1902 encounter at Leyton, but Ranji's powers of persuasion had triumphed and it turned out to be a wholly historic occasion. Sussex had not made a good start at all on the Monday morning and Ranji, who had by his own standards been experiencing a rather indifferent season – although he eventually topped the County's Championship batting averages – found himself at the crease with 4 wickets down for 82 runs. They were soon to be 6 wickets down for 92 runs, but at this point Newham, batting at number eight – a position much lower than the one he occupied in his heyday – joined the maestro. The duo, to quote the *Brighton Herald,* 'brought about a change in the aspect of the game that is rarely known, even in the glorious uncertainty of cricket.'

At the end of the first day, with the Sussex total on 424 for 6 wickets, Newham had reached 146 and Ranji 184 – his only errors were a stumping chance on 23 and a chance to the wicketkeeper on 176 – and the partnership was still going strong. The two continued on the Tuesday morning, and by the time they were parted, they had added 344 for the seventh wicket – at the time a world record and even today a record for this wicket in English cricket. They had been together for four hours and twenty minutes and Sussex had reached a strong position by scoring 520. The *Brighton Herald* reporter was effusive in his praise: 'Each in their different ways played superb cricket, Ranjitsinhji in that fascinating meteoric style that is peculiarly his own, exhibiting pretty well every kind of good stroke to perfection, while Mr Newham got his runs in his quieter, but eminently sound and sturdy fashion.'

Rain, however, that blight of English cricket, intervened by bringing the players off just before four o'clock, with Essex on 101 for 2 wickets. On the Wednesday, the last day, the extrovert Essex amateur, Charlie McGahey, played with great skill and forestalled any form of collapse by his side, while Fred Tate bowled commendably, taking 6 wickets and conceding fewer than 2 runs per over. Although Essex in the end were forced to follow-on, sound batting by Frederick Fane and Edward Sewell finally secured a creditable draw for their team.

Billy Newham first played for Sussex in 1881, served both as captain and secretary and, in the course of a long and fruitful cricket life, contributed to the welfare of the County for more than sixty years. Even in 1944, the year of his death, he was still helping out with the secretarial work at Hove.

Ranjitsinhji scored a massive 230 in a partnership of 344.

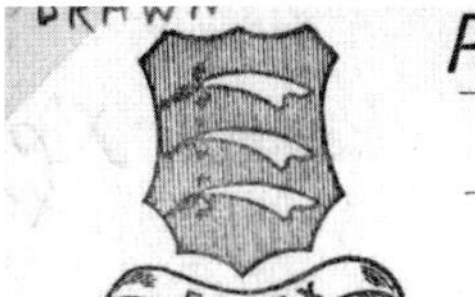

PRICE 1d. [Printed on the Ground by PHELP BROTHERS, Leyton and Walthamstow.] 1902

ESSEX COUNTY CRICKET CLUB, LEYTON.

ESSEX v. SUSSEX,

Monday, Tuesday & Wednesday, June 30 and July 1 & 2

STUMPS DRAWN 6.30 EACH DAY. UMPIRES WRIGHT AND WHITE.

SUSSEX.	FIRST INNINGS.		SECOND INNINGS.	
1 C. B. FRY	c Kortright b Young	15		
2 VINE	c Russell b Young	12		
3 KILLICK	c Kortright b McGahey	30		
4 RELF A.E.	b Mead	9		
5 MARLOW	c Russell b Young	10		
6 K. S. RANJITSINHJI	c Sewell b McGahey	230		
7 G. BRANN	b McGahey	0		
8 W. NEWHAM	c Carpenter b Mead	153		
9 TATE	c Russell b Mead	5		
10 BUTT	not out	29		
11 CORDINGLEY	b McGahey	3		
Extras	b 18, l.b 2, w 2, n.b 2,	24	b , l.b. , w , n.b ,	
TOTAL		520	TOTAL	

FALL OF WICKETS—FIRST INNINGS. SECOND INNINGS.

	1	2	3	4	5	6	7	8	9	10
First innings	17	49	67	82	92	92	436	448	503	520
Second innings	...	...	..	...	..	...	...	...	...	...

BOWLING ANALYSIS.

FIRST INNINGS.	Ovs.	Mds.	Rs.	Wks.	Wds.	Nbs.	SECOND INNINGS.	Ovs.	Mds.	Rs.	Wks.	Wds.	Nbs.
Mead	37	5	129	3	...	...		...	...	...	...	...	...
Young	41	7	131	3	1	2		...	...	...	...	...	...
McGahey	31.1	8	57	4	...		Kortright	4	0	23	0	...	...
Reeves	8	0	48	0	...		Sewell	9	1	20	0	...	..
Tosetti	19	3	51	0	...		Carpenter	2	0	7	0	...	...
Buckenham	7	1	30	0	..	...		...	...	...	...	...	...

ESSEX.	FIRST INNINGS.		SECOND INNINGS.	
1 1 F. L. FANE	c Butt b Tate	31	not out	69
2 2 CARPENTER	c sub b Tate	35	c Cordingley b Tate	16
4 3 C. McGAHEY	run out	104		
4 G. TOSETTI	run out	0		
5 C. J. KORTRIGHT	c sub b Tate	9	c Cordingley b Brann	99
3 6 SEWELL	c Relf b Tate	10		
7 RUSSELL (T.)	c sub b Relf	47		
8 BUCKENHAM	c Cordingley b Tate	1		
9 YOUNG	not out	3		
10 REEVES	lbw b Tate	6		
11 MEAD	c Butt b Relf	2		
Extras	b 10, l.b 6, w , n.b. 2,	18	b 2, l.b 1, w , n.b	3
TOTAL		266	TOTAL (2 wkts)	187

FALL OF WICKETS—FIRST INNINGS. SECOND INNINGS.

	1	2	3	4	5	6	7	8	9	10
First innings	43	57	117	135	139	139	243	261	261	266
Second innings	18	187	...	...	...	...	...	...	...	...

BOWLING ANALYSIS.

FIRST INNINGS.	Ovs.	Mds.	Rs.	Wks.	Wds.	Nbs.	SECOND INNINGS. Ovs.	Mds.	Rs.	Wks.	Wds.	Nbs
Tate	51	14	96	6	...	1	18	7	42	1	...	...
A.E. Relf	19.1	6	65	2	...	...	12	4	22	0	...	1
Killick	16	8	22	0	...	1	8	0	48	0	...	...
Vine	11	1	35	0	...	...	...	...	...	...	...	..
Cordingley	12	3	30	0	...	...	5	0	21	0	...	..
Brann	...	...		...	...	...	8	0	51	1	...	...

NEXT MATCH AT LEYTON— **ESSEX v. AUSTRALIANS**

MONDAY, TUESDAY & WEDNESDAY, JULY 28, 29 & 30.

SUSSEX *v.* SURREY

14, 15 and 16 July 1902 County Championship
Hastings

Between 1900 and 1905, with Ranjitsinhji and Charles Fry in charge of the County's fortunes, Sussex were constantly near the top of the Championship – they finished twice in second place, twice in third place and only once as low as sixth. In 1902, when they reached second place behind Yorkshire, they also achieved their highest innings total, which remains a record today.

The Hastings ground, now sadly a shopping mall and sorely missed by many a Sussex cricketer, provided the venue for a match in which the bat wholly dominated the ball and led to a total of 1,427 runs being scored – a record at the time for a first-class match in England. On the Monday morning, Charles Fry and Joe Vine, the latter no doubt under orders from Fry to play steadily while his imperious partner attacked the bowling, put together 238 for the first wicket and, although Billy Newham and George Brann, who had both scored hundreds against Yorkshire in the previous match, were out to successive balls, the County reached 419 for 6 wickets at the close of play.

Tuesday saw George Cox help Ranji, who had been 54* overnight, to add 192 in one hundred minutes and this was followed by a further unbeaten stand – 160 in seventy minutes between Ranji and Fred Tate, the former having played a chanceless innings in three hours and twenty-five minutes and having hit 39 fours. At this point, with the 700 reached, Ranji felt that it was time for Surrey to bat. The visitors were not averse to performing on such a good wicket, and Tom Hayward and Bobby Abel took the Surrey total to 246 before the first wicket fell. At the close on that day, with Surrey on 275 for 1 wicket, a total of 980 runs had been scored in two days for the loss of only 9 wickets.

On the Wednesday, the match became more of a display of magnificent batsmanship than a keenly fought contest. Captain Bush helped Abel raise the Surrey total to 443 before the second wicket fell, but the rest of the batting was less productive and the innings closed on 552. In practice, Ranji could have enforced the follow-on, but decided to let his batsmen enjoy themselves on the perfect wicket as the game drew to a close.

Ranji, playing in only 11 Championship matches in 1902, was easily the County's leading batsman, two of his three centuries passing the two-hundred mark, but he caused some grumbling among the members owing to his appearing in fewer than half the Championship games after rumours of differences with some professionals. For all that, he captained the side well and, as Harry Altham once noted: 'It is an open secret, which he himself would be the first to admit, that it was his association with the Indian Prince that raised Charles Fry from a good into a great player.'

An early picture of Hastings – a popular ground with Sussex players over the years.

Sussex won the toss and elected to bat

SUSSEX

Mr C.B. Fry	c Brockwell b Dowson	159		
J. Vine	c Dowson b Richardson	92	b Jephson	7
E.H. Killick	lbw b Clode	41	not out	18
A.E. Relf	c and b Dowson	20	c and b Dowson	77
*K.S. Ranjitsinhji	not out	234		
Mr W. Newham	c and b Dowson	2		
Mr G. Brann	lbw b Dowson	0	b Hayes	48
G. Cox	c Hayes b Clode	51		
#H.R. Butt	c Hayward b Dowson	6		
F.W. Tate	not out	61		
C.H.G. Bland	did not bat		st Stedman b Hayes	13
Extras	(b 25, lb 9, nb 5)	39	(b 5, lb 1, nb 1)	7
TOTAL	(for 8 wkts dec.)	705	(for 4 wkts)	170

Bowling	O	M	R	W	O	M	R	W
Lockwood	24	5	98	0				
Richardson	30	1	143	1				
Clode	35	3	129	2				
Brockwell	21	1	99	0	11	2	40	0
Dowson	28	4	137	5	7	1	44	1
Jephson	16	1	36	0	14	5	59	1
Hayes	8	1	24	0	5.1	1	11	2
Bush					1	0	9	0

SURREY

R. Abel	c Cox b Bland	179
T. Hayward	c Bland b Tate	144
Capt H.S. Bush	C Ranjitsinhji b Tate	122
E.G. Hayes	lbw b Cox	42
W. Brockwell	c Butt b Tate	5
Mr E.M. Dowson	b Cox	0
*Mr D.L.A. Jephson	not out	43
H. Clode	c Killick b Tate	11
#A. Stedman	b Bland	2
T. Richardson	b Bland	0
W.H. Lockwood	absent ill	
Extras	(b 4)	4
TOTAL		552

Bowling	O	M	R	W
Vine	27	7	77	0
Bland	29.3	4	98	3
Cox	40	14	149	2
Relf	11	0	69	0
Tate	48	11	155	4

Umpires:
T. Mycroft and F. Martin

Match Drawn

SUSSEX *v.* YORKSHIRE

8, 9 and 10 June 1903 — County Championship
Bradford

Yorkshire *aficionados* will doubtless claim, almost certainly with some justification, that their side has achieved more victories in matches with Sussex than has been the reverse case, but 1903 happened not be one of those seasons. In this match, Sussex sent the Tykes packing with an innings victory and, in the return game at Hove, the County overcame them by 4 wickets, albeit with something of a struggle.

The Bradford encounter was Yorkshire's first home match of the season. In truth they had not done badly up till then, having defeated Essex, Gloucestershire and Cambridge University and having lost only twice. They came to Bradford with a team slightly below par: George Hirst was out with a damaged calf muscle and John Tunnicliffe, in catching Joe Vine early in the Sussex innings, re-opened an old wound and was ruled out for the remainder of the match. For all that, Sussex proved wholly the better side.

Ranjitsinhji won the toss and the Sussex innings was opened by Charles Fry and Vine. Although the latter went early, Ernest Killick weighed in with a half-century and, when Ranji joined Fry, they put together a third-wicket partnership of 174 in two hours. At the close on the opening day, with Fry undefeated on 160, Sussex were well placed at 337 for 3 wickets. The Yorkshire bowlers, missing the guile of Hirst, had appeared to experience a certain lack of confidence and tended to bowl wide of the off-stump, thus attempting to cut down on Fry's prolific leg-side scoring. While it is true that he scored more heavily on that side of the wicket, he was certainly not short of strokes elsewhere. In fact, when he was once criticised for having only one stroke, he replied: 'True, but I can send it in twenty-two places.'

Charles Fry – his record was not beaten until 1991.

The second day saw Fry go on to his double hundred – his 234 remained Sussex's highest score against Yorkshire until beaten eighty-eight years later by Alan Wells' 253* in 1991 – and, when he was out with the County's score on 466, he had been at the wicket for nearly seven hours. After half-centuries had been recorded by Billy Newham and George Cox, the closure was applied at lunch-time. In just over two hours, Yorkshire were bundled out for 120, their fifth lowest total of the season – two of the lower ones were their 72 and 96 against Sussex at Hove – and, after they had been forced to follow-on, they had lost Stanley Jackson in their second innings before the close.

The Tykes did rather better in their second knock. David Denton, sometimes known as 'Lucky', batted skilfully for his 51 and Lord Hawke's unbeaten half-century kept the Sussex attack at bay for some hours. In the end, however, there was no doubting who were the convincing winners. In the days of Sussex's 'Golden Age' in the early 1900s, they were certainly a team to contend with.

Sussex won the toss and elected to bat

SUSSEX

Mr C.B. Fry	lbw b Jackson	234
J. Vine	c Tunnicliffe b Haigh	13
E.H. Killick	c Hunter b Jackson	58
*K.S. Ranjitsinhji	c Hunter b Denton	93
A.E. Relf	c Jackson b Rhodes	19
Mr C.L.A. Smith	c Jackson b Rhodes	11
Mr W. Newham	c and b Wainwright	59
G. Cox	b Wainwright	55
#H.R. Butt	not out	4
F.W. Tate, C.H.G. Bland did not bat		
Extras	(b8, lb4)	12
TOTAL	(for 8 wkts dec.)	558

Bowling	O	M	R	W
Rhodes	57	12	135	2
Jackson	34	12	125	2
Haigh	54	8	157	1
Wainwright	35	4	73	2
Whitehead	9	0	31	0
Denton	9	0	25	1

YORKSHIRE

Hon F.S. Jackson	c Ranjitsinhji b Relf	7	b Cox	20
J.T. Brown	c Tate b Relf	0	b Relf	20
D. Denton	b Relf	15	b Tate	51
F. Smith	b Cox	6	c Tate b Relf	22
L. Whitehead	b Cox	13	c Tate b Relf	12
*Lord Hawke	c Tate b Cox	26	not out	61
W. Rhodes	b Cox	0	lbw b Tate	2
S. Haigh	c Fry b Killick	17	c and b Tate	1
W. Wainwright	c Fry b Killick	24	c Butt b Cox	26
#D. Hunter	not out	2	c Butt b Bland	20
J. Tunnicliffe	absent hurt		absent hurt	
Extras	(b5, lb1, nb3, w1)	10	(b14, lb8, w1)	23
TOTAL		120		258

Bowling	O	M	R	W	O	M	R	W
Relf	22	4	47	3	40	17	68	3
Bland	7	0	20	0	20	5	39	1
Cox	16	4	40	4	25.1	10	46	2
Killick	2	1	3	2				
Tate					28	11	53	3
Ranjitsinhji					7	3	17	0
Vine					7	3	12	0

Umpires: R.G. Barlow and W. Attewell

Sussex won by an innings and 180 runs

SUSSEX v. MIDDLESEX

28 and 29 June 1906 — County Championship
Hove

In 1906 awards for the Man of the Match did not exist, but had they done so there can be little doubt that Elicius Benedict Dwyer – he had, in fact, seven forenames, but finally settled on two – would have been the recipient in Sussex's match with Middlesex in 1906. Ben Dwyer's great-grandfather, a Wicklow chieftain, had been deported to Australia in 1798 and he himself had been born in Sydney in 1876, only later coming to live in England. He played for the County for six seasons between 1904 and 1909, but only in two – 1906 and 1907 – did his fast-medium bowling achieve significant results.

In their second match of the season, Sussex had been beaten by Middlesex by 4 wickets at Lord's, so the return match at Hove was not without point. Charles Fry had been injured at Lord's and, to quote the *Brighton Herald*, 'there was no news of Ranjitsinhji'. The fact, therefore, that Middlesex were under-represented was compensated for by the Sussex absentees. Charles Smith, deputising for Fry, lost the toss and Middlesex, despite a somewhat foggy morning with some drizzle, which meant that the first ball was not bowled until just after noon, decided to bat in front of a meagre crowd. The Middlesex batsmen were almost immediately at sea against the opening attack of Dwyer and Albert Relf, and five minutes after lunch, when the visitors' last man, Mignon, was caught by George Leach in the deep, their innings was over. Sussex did not have things all their own way either, and Smith and Joe Vine were quickly dismissed, but Ernest Killick and Albert Relf steadied the innings and added 90 runs before the latter was caught. Although the amateur Ernest Read failed to trouble the scorers, Robert Relf was unbeaten on 57 and George Cox on 19 when the close came.

Rain fell steadily on Thursday night and into Friday morning, so there was a long delay before play got underway at 3.10 p.m. Robert Relf was soon caught at mid-off, but useful contributions by Cox and Leach saw the County's total reach 286, a handsome lead of 190 runs. The Middlesex batsmen were again quite unable to cope with Dwyer and Albert Relf on what was largely a treacherous pitch, and 7 wickets had soon fallen for 38 runs. Although MacGregor and Baker offered some resistance, Dwyer, keeping an excellent length and varying his pace cleverly, was carrying all before him and the visitors soon succumbed to defeat by an innings and 101 runs. Dwyer's 16 wickets remained a Sussex record until George Cox took 17 against Warwickshire in 1926, but to this day he remains in second place. 1906 and 1907 were very much his best period for in these two seasons he took 154 of the 179 wickets that he totalled in his career for Sussex.

John Dwyer – a fast bowler who was originally from Australia.

Middlesex won the toss and elected to bat

MIDDLESEX

F.A. Tarrant	c R.R.Relf b Dwyer	13	b Dwyer	13
Mr W.P. Harrison	b A.E. Relf	12	b A.E. Relf	3
Mr J.H. Stogdon	b A.E. Relf	3	b Dwyer	0
J.T. Rawlin	c Butt b A.E.Relf	1	b Dwyer	0
A.E. Trott	b Dwyer	13	c Cox b Dwyer	0
Mr C.P. Foley	c Butt b Dwyer	0	b Dwyer	9
*#Mr G. MacGregor	c R.R. Relf b Dwyer	0	c A.E. Relf b Dwyer	11
Mr C.V. Baker	b Dwyer	1	not out	28
Mr C.B.W. Magnay	st Butt b Dwyer	7	b Dwyer	1
J.T. Hearne	not out	28	lbw b Dwyer	4
E. Mignon	c Leach b Dwyer	8	b Dwyer	2
Extras	(b4, lb5, w1)	10	(b12, lb2, nb4)	18
TOTAL		96		89

Bowling	O	M	R	W	O	M	R	W
Dwyer	21.3	5	56	7	23.3	11	44	9
A.E. Relf	21	8	30	3	15	11	12	1
Killick					8	4	15	0

SUSSEX

*Mr C.L.A. Smith	b Rawlin	4
J. Vine	c MacGregor b Mignon	0
E.H. Killick	c Hearne b Trott	96
A.E. Relf	c Trott b Hearne	40
R.R. Relf	c Mignon b Tarrant	58
Mr E.G. Read	b Trott	0
G. Cox	b Tarrant	32
G. Leach	run out	27
Mr H .L. Simms	not out	13
E. B. Dwyer	c Stogdon b Trott	9
#H.R. Butt	c and b Tarrant	0
Extras	(b4, lb 3)	7
TOTAL		286

Bowling	O	M	R	W
Rawlin	8	2	24	1
Mignon	13	0	65	1
Trott	19	5	75	3
Hearne	28	6	63	1
Tarrant	22.2	4	50	3
Magnay	1	0	2	0

Umpires: J. Carlin and R.G. Barlow

Sussex won by an innings and 101 runs

Sussex v. Kent

5, 6 and 7 August 1907 — County Championship
Canterbury

The 66th Canterbury Week opened in fine weather in August 1907. Sussex were not enjoying the best of seasons and, in their encounter with Kent in May, they had lost by an innings. For this match, in what proved to be an inspired move, they had brought in Robert Relf. Having won the toss, they made a disastrous start, losing Joe Vine and Dick Young for ducks and, although Charles Fry batted well, they had collapsed to 90 for 6 wickets by lunch. Soon afterwards, John Nason was dismissed and it was left to Robert Relf, assisted by the two Georges – Cox and Leach – to take the County's total beyond the 200-mark. Leach hit his 30, made from 37 while he was at the wicket, in twenty minutes, but by tea 9 wickets were down. One ball afterwards and it was all over, and Relf was left stranded on 67. Sussex fought back, however, and by the close Kent had lost 3 wickets for 63.

Despite rain overnight, play began on time at 11.20 a.m. the next day, and by lunch Kent had moved on to 185 for 7 wickets. After lunch the crowds poured into the ground, and it was reckoned that over 7,000 people watched the continuation of play. If Sussex thought that they had fought back, they were, sadly, in error. They had not reckoned on the Kent captain, Jack Mason, whose century helped to give his side a lead of 143 runs. Vine and Young opened the Sussex second innings and were batting well when Young was dismissed with twenty minutes to go. Fry was padded up ready to bat, but suddenly changed his mind. Through a pavilion window, he apparently shouted: 'Where's young Relf? You're in now!' Relf, expecting to bat no higher than number eight, had changed out of his whites and had to hurriedly change back so that, when he reached the wicket, the Kent fielders were muttering about the two-minute rule. Vine and Relf were half-amused and half-annoyed at their skipper's peremptory behaviour and decided to keep him waiting.

The following morning, Vine and Relf were still together at lunch, and only some time afterwards was Vine, having completed his third hundred that season, finally dismissed. *Wisden*, certainly unaware of the pact, noted that 'the partnership became very tedious towards the close'. With Fry now batting, Relf, who had taken three hours to reach his first hundred, then proceeded to score another 110 in barely seventy minutes! Fry's declaration left Kent ninety minutes to score 344 and the match was drawn. It is not sure whether Fry knew that he had been taught a lesson, but Relf had scored his first double hundred and, later in the day, received the following telegram from Brighton: 'Hearty congratulations from Godfrey senior [a committee member]. I have given 'Leather Hunter' [A.J. Gaston, a Sussex cricket journalist] a handsome pipe for you in recognition of your brilliant 200.'

JOE
VINE
STILL IN
J'Y SUIS . J'Y RESTE

Joe Vine – the cartoon jokes about his slow scoring.

Sussex won the toss and elected to bat

SUSSEX

*Mr C.B. Fry	st Huish b Mason	39	(4) not out	37
J. Vine	c Mason b Woolley	0	c Mason b Woolley	108
#Mr R.A. Young	b Woolley	0	(2) b Dillon	60
E.H. Killick	c Seymour b Fielder	12		
Mr J.W. Nason	b Fielder	25		
A.E. Relf	c Mason b Humphreys	0		
Mr C.L.A. Smith	b Humphreys	0		
R.R. Relf	not out	67	(3) c Seymour b Dillon	210
G. Cox	b Humphreys	34		
G. Leach	c Day b Fairservice	30		
E .B. Dwyer	run out	0		
Extras	(lb1, nb2)	3	(b15, lb2, w4)	21
TOTAL		210	(for 3 wkts dec.)	486

Bowling	O	M	R	W	O	M	R	W
Fielder	23	4	75	2	26	7	75	0
Woolley	19	3	44	2	20	3	69	1
Humphreys	13	2	42	3	23	10	50	0
Mason	11	6	24	1	15	3	52	0
Fairservice	5.5	1	22	1	21	6	56	0
Dillon					16.4	3	58	2
Seymour					11	4	46	0
Blaker					1	0	9	0

KENT

Mr E.W. Dillon	c R.R. Relf b A.E. Relf	9		
E. Humphreys	run out	9	not out	10
James Seymour	run out	36		
Mr K.L. Hutchings	c Leach b A.E. Relf	32		
Mr S.H. Day	c Young b Cox	3	not out	60
F.E. Woolley	c Cox b Leach	15	st Young b Killick	11
*Mr J.R. Mason	not out	121		
Mr R.N.R. Blaker	c Young b Killick	19	b Leach	23
#F.H. Huish	c Young b Leach	39	b Leach	6
W.J. Fairservice	c and b Killick	50		
A. Fielder	b A.E. Relf	11		
Extras	(lb 9)	9	(b1, nb1)	2
TOTAL		353	(for 3 wkts)	112

Bowling	O	M	R	W	O	M	R	W
Cox	31	10	89	1				
A.E. Relf	34.1	11	105	3				
Dwyer	9	0	31	0	1	0	5	0
Leach	18	4	67	2	16	1	52	2
Killick	19	4	52	2	15	3	53	1

Umpires: F.G. Roberts and J.E. West

Match Drawn

Sussex *v.* Nottinghamshire

18, 19 and 20 May 1911 — County Championship
Hove

Later cricketers have played some glorious innings, but the most astounding assault on any bowling still remains Edwin Alletson's 189 in ninety minutes against Sussex in May 1911. Twenty-seven at the time, Alletson was the son of a wheelwright on the estate of the Duke of Portland in Nottinghamshire. Broad-shouldered and powerful, he had acquired something of a reputation as a hitter, but he was regarded more as a bowler than a batsman and had enjoyed no significant success until this time. In fact, he played in this match only because Tom Wass was unfit, while he himself was nursing a sprained wrist and was barely passed fit. The match began innocently enough on a Thursday morning. Nottinghamshire, on winning the toss, decided to bat on the habitually placid Hove wicket and, despite some early losses, the two hours before lunch saw them reach 148 for 3 wickets. George Gunn was in excellent form and helped the visitors reach 190 with only 4 wickets down. At this point, however, Charles Smith introduced Ernest Killick into the attack and his slow-medium pace was so effective that he took 5 wickets in no time at all, and Nottinghamshire succumbed to 238 all out. This left Sussex ninety minutes' batting in which Robert Relf and Joe Vine rattled up 74 for the first wicket in sixty-five minutes, and the County ended the day on 117 for 1 wicket.

On the Friday, Sussex, at 198 for 5, looked unlikely to secure a substantial lead, but Killick, batting lower than normal at number seven, came to the rescue with a fluent 81 and took Sussex past the 400-mark by 4.00 p.m. After the loss of an early wicket, the visitors batted soundly to reach 152 for 3 at the close. On the Saturday morning, the Relf brothers were soon amongst the Nottinghamshire batsmen and the visitors were quickly reduced to 185 for 7. At this point Ted Alletson came to the wicket. In the remaining fifty minutes before lunch, he scored a responsible 47, which in no way presaged the fireworks that were to follow. A further two wickets fell before lunch, which left opening bowler William Riley as his last partner and the score on 262 for 9.

The Sussex dining-room must have provided Alletson with an excellent lunch, for after the interval, the character of his innings changed completely. Treating the bowling of Killick and Leach like that of schoolboys, he took 9 runs off each of their first overs, then hit Killick for 22 and Leach

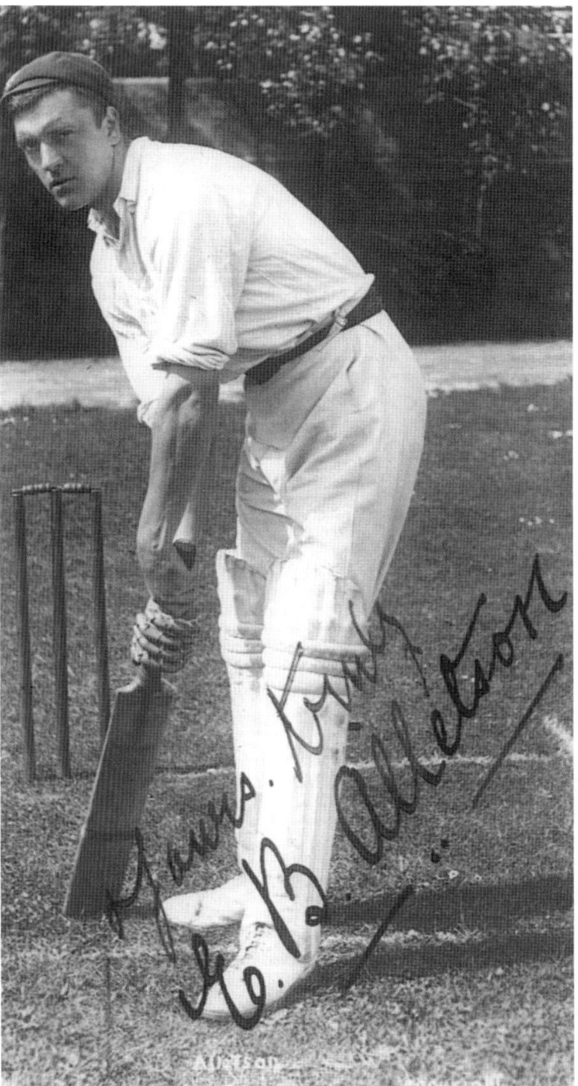

Ted Alletson, the mighty Nottinghamshire hitter.

Nottinghamshire won the toss and elected to bat

NOTTINGHAMSHIRE

*Mr A.O. Jones	b Cox	57	b Leach	0
J. Iremonger	c and b A.E. Relf	0	c Tudor b Killick	83
G. Gunn	st Butt b Cox	90	st Butt b R.R. Relf	66
J. Hardstaff	b Cox	8	c Butt b A.E. Relf	7
J. R. Gunn	c R.R. Relf b Killick	33	b R.R. Relf	19
W. Payton	c Heygate b Killick	20	lbw b A.E. Relf	0
W.W. Whysall	b Killick	1	c Butt b A.E. Relf	3
G.M. Lee	c and b Killick	10	c Cox b Leach	26
E. B. Alletson	c Killick b A.E. Relf	7	c Smith b Cox	189
#T. Oates	not out	3	b Leach	1
W. Riley	c Smith b Killick	3	not out	10
Extras	(b5, nb 1)	6	(b3, lb2, w2, nb1)	8
TOTAL		238		412

Bowling	O	M	R	W	O	M	R	W
A.E. Relf	19	5	40	2	33	13	92	3
Leach	11	2	53	0	19	2	91	3
Vincett	4	0	31	0	3	1	25	0
R.R. Relf	11	0	36	0	19	6	39	2
Cox	25	4	58	3	9.4	2	27	1
Killick	10.2	4	14	5	20	2	130	1

SUSSEX

R.R. Relf	b Jones	42	c Oates b Jones	71
J. Vine	b Jones	77	c Payton b Riley	54
Mr R.B. Heygate	c Lee b Iremonger	32	b J.R. Gunn	13
G. Cox	c Alletson b Riley	37	st Oates b Riley	5
A.E. Relf	c and b Jones	4	c Oates b Riley	0
Mr C.L. Tudor	c Oates b Riley	23	b J.R. Gunn	4
E.H. Killick	c Hardstaff b Lee	81	c Lee b Riley	21
G. Leach	b Lee	52	b J.R. Gunn	31
*Mr C.L.A. Smith	not out	33	not out	12
J.H. Vincett	c Iremonger b Lee	9	not out	1
#H.R. Butt	b Riley	13		
Extras	(b4, lb3, w1, nb3)	11	(nb1)	1
TOTAL		414	(for 8 wkts)	213

Bowling	O	M	R	W	O	M	R	W
Iremonger	34	7	97	1	14	2	34	0
Riley	29.4	5	102	3	33	9	82	4
J.R. Gunn	29	2	87	0	25	9	41	3
Jones	22	2	69	3	5	1	24	1
Alletson	1	0	3	0				
Lee	14	1	45	3	4	0	31	0

Umpires: H. Wood and A.A. White

Match Drawn

Joe Vine helped give Sussex a good start in both innings.

Ernest Killick was hit for 34 in one over.

for 13. Having scored his second fifty in twenty minutes, he reached his hundred after seventy-five minutes, but even this was small beer compared to that which followed. Killick, bowling two no-balls, disappeared for 34 in 1 over and in the 7 overs after lunch, Alletson had made 115 runs out of 120 scored. Robert Relf then went for 15 in 1 over and by the time George Cox, having twice been dispatched for 4 near square-leg, had him caught he had scored his last 89 runs in fifteen minutes. Alletson's wonderful innings came mainly from tremendous drives so that his 189 contained 8 sixes, 23 fours, 4 threes, 10 twos and only 17 singles. No fewer than 6 of the sixes were prodigious straight drives clean over the stand, another smashed the pavilion clock and another a window and part of the bar. Of the 152 runs added in 65 balls after lunch, he had received 51 of them and scored 142 runs in forty minutes.

Sussex, who at one stage must have thought that they would need only a few runs to win, found themselves needing 237 in three-and-a-quarter hours for victory. Although Robert Relf and Joe Vine gave the County a brilliant start, scoring 112 in seventy-five minutes, the middle order failed to match them and, at one point, 6 men were out for 148. Sussex then put up the shutters and played out time until 6.30 p.m. What might have been an easy victory nearly became a disastrous defeat.

It is said that every dog has his day and this was surely Alletson's. He stayed with Nottinghamshire for a further three seasons, but never scored another century, although he hit Wilfred Rhodes for 3 consecutive sixes in the course of making 35 against Yorkshire at Dewsbury in 1913. Having served in the Royal Garrison Artillery in the First World War, he left cricket and became a miner at the Manton Colliery.

SUSSEX *v.* LANCASHIRE

24, 25 and 26 July 1913 County Championship
Horsham

Sussex had beaten Lancashire by 5 wickets only a few days previously at Old Trafford in the 1913 season, but during the greater part of the return match at Horsham, they were on the receiving end of the Tyldesley brothers' batting and the Northerners' excellent attack. The second match of the Horsham Cricket Week began in fine weather, although the pitch was reckoned to be on the soft side. This induced Herbert Chaplin to ask his opponents to take the first innings. Albert Relf and Norman Holloway made good use of the conditions, and Lancashire lost three early wickets which pegged their scoring back, Holloway at one stage bowling 10 overs and conceding merely 3 singles. Despite Chaplin's constant bowling changes, John and Ernest Tyldesley formed a productive partnership and Joe Vine, in particular, was roughly handled. After lunch, the wicket started to play much more easily, and the brothers' partnership continued until John Tyldesley was caught by George Cox at first slip off Albert Relf. The pair had added 149 for the fourth wicket in two and a quarter hours. After Ernest had reached his half-century and had been smartly caught by Chaplin at mid-off, the innings subsided and Sussex, who reached 16 for no wicket at the close, must have felt that they had enjoyed a productive day.

The weather was again fine on Friday morning, but the Sussex batsmen were in total disarray against the bowling of William Huddleston and Harry Dean, the former's medium-pace off-spin extracting much more life than the Sussex bowlers had been able to achieve. The County's batsmen, who had taken two hours and ten minutes to reach a modest 81, had made exceptionally heavy weather of their innings and, 6 runs short of the required total, were asked to follow-on. Although they made a very slow start to their second knock, Vine (who completed his 1,000 runs for the season) and Herbert Wilson made steady progress, and good contributions by the Relfs brought the County to 177 for 4 wickets by the close – a modest lead of 22 runs.

Saturday dawned dull and uninviting and the not-out batsmen, Chaplin and Percy Fender, made slow progress against the Lancashire bowling, which was supported by brilliant fielding. Although wickets continued to go down regularly, a brilliant 71 in eighty minutes by wicketkeeper Arthur Lang, the twenty-two-year-old Cambridge University blue, altered the course of the innings which ended on a respectable 332. Set 178 to win, Lancashire batted stolidly and reached 83 for 5 wickets at tea. The match was starting to go Sussex's way and, after the interval, the remaining 5 wickets went down quickly so that Sussex completed their double over the northern county. *Wisden* saw the match as 'wonderfully interesting from start to finish' and the result meant that Sussex, and not Lancashire, occupied seventh place in the final County Championship table.

Sussex at Horsham in 1913.

Sussex won the toss and elected to field

LANCASHIRE

*Mr A.H. Hornby	b A.E. Relf	3	lbw b Vincett	29
H. Makepeace	lbw b Holloway	1	c Vincett b A.E. Relf	17
J.T. Tyldesley	c Cox b A.E. Relf	107	c Vincett b A.E. Relf	15
J. Sharp	b Holloway	1	lbw b Vincett	4
E. Tyldesley	c Chaplin b Cox	57	c Vincett b A.E. Relf	10
Mr K.G. McLeod	b Holloway	16	c A.E. Relf b Vincett	7
J.S. Heap	c Fender b A.E. Relf	5	c Lang b A.E. Relf	0
R. Whitehead	b A.E. Relf	0	b Vincett	12
#Mr R.A. Boddington	not out	11	lbw b Vincett	0
W. Huddleston	c Cartwright A.E. Relf	23	b A.E. Relf	8
H. Dean	b A.E. Relf	0	not out	1
Extras	(b11, w1)	12	(b4, lb5)	9
TOTAL		236		112

Bowling	O	M	R	W	O	M	R	W
A.E. Relf	37.1	18	56	6	28	13	52	5
Holloway	20	11	24	3	10	2	26	0
Vine	2	0	20	0				
Cox	23	7	38	1				
Vincett	13	1	34	0	17	7	25	5
Fender	8	1	31	0				
Wilson	3	0	21	0				

SUSSEX

Mr H.L. Wilson	b Huddleston	13	b Huddleston	20
J. Vine	lbw b Huddleston	13	b Heap	23
R.R. Relf	lbw b Huddleston	7	c Hornby b Dean	51
A.E. Relf	c Boddington b Dean	1	lbw b Huddlesaton	28
Mr P. Cartwright	b Huddleston	0	b Huddleston	4
Mr P.G.H. Fender	b Dean	1	b Heap	49
*Mr H.P. Chaplin	not out	13	b Dean	26
#Mr A.H. Lang	c Huddleston b Dean	13	lbw b Huddleston	71
G. Cox	b Dean	0	lbw b Dean	21
J. H. Vincett	lbw b Huddleston	8	c J.T. Tyldesley b Dean	8
Mr N.J. Holloway	b Huddleston	4	not out	7
Extras	(b4, lb4)	8	(b12, lb12)	24
TOTAL		81		332

Bowling	O	M	R	W	O	M	R	W
Whitehead	5	2	9	0	13	6	26	0
Huddleston	20.1	12	22	6	59	22	104	4
Dean	22	11	42	4	54.3	17	125	4
Heap					20	3	53	2

Umpires: A.E. Trott and G. Webb

Sussex won by 65 runs

SUSSEX *v.* SOMERSET

21 and 22 May 1919 County Championship
Taunton

The First World War had ended barely six months previously when cricket was resumed in May 1919. In the circumstances, it was decided to restrict all County matches to two days, and to let the result of the Championship be determined by the percentage of actual wins to matches played, thus robbing the competition of much of its significance and leading to a multitude of drawn games in what proved to be a particularly dry summer.

Few matches in terms of the innings totals can have been as close as the early season Sussex – Somerset clash at Taunton. Sussex fielded an unfamiliar side with Chaplin, Vine, the Relf brothers, Jupp, Street and Bowley all missing from the pre-war XI. The Somerset innings was opened by the Rippon twins – Londoners who had attended King's College, Taunton – and, although Sydney went for 26, Dudley played well for his 60, while Hope, the Bath rugby captain, and Bridges hit hard and landed at least one ball in the River Tone. George Cox, however, bowled steadily and had claimed 5 wickets by the time the home side were all out for 243. He had been aided by some good wicket-keeping by Robert Miller, a pre-war Uppingham schoolboy who had been drafted into the County side in Street's absence.

Sussex's first innings was built around the batting of Herbert Wilson, who had been asked to take over the captaincy in this first post-war season. His 56 and a stout 69 from Maurice Tate, batting at eight, meant that the County ended up only one run short of the Somerset total. When Somerset batted again, they struggled against the Sussex attack and George Cox, by now turning the ball sharply and aided by Roberts and Vincett, rattled the home side out for 103 on the second morning. Sussex certainly looked as though they were in the driving seat, as chasing 105, even on the unpredictable Taunton wicket, did not look too formidable a task. Harold Heygate, who had batted at number eleven and failed to score in the Sussex first innings and who had not fielded in the second Somerset knock, was said to be crippled by rheumatism and unable to bat, even if required. While Herbert Wilson again played a captain's innings, wickets fell regularly at the other end, so that the County found themselves at 104 for 9 with the scores level and the skipper still there on 42*. The thirty-four-year-old Heygate was now pressed into batting and, besuited and with pads hastily strapped on, he emerged from the pavilion after about four minutes, only to find that umpire Street had pulled up the stumps under Law 45 and declared him 'timed out'. There was then some confusion about the result, but the scores were level and a tie was agreed upon. A later appeal to Lord's upheld the umpires, although *Wisden* was not impressed, it seems, referring to 'an extraordinary and in some respects very regrettable incident'.

Herbert Heygate – 'timed out'.

Somerset won the toss and elected to bat

SOMERSET

Mr A.E.S. Rippon	c Miller b Stannard	26	b Cox	8
Mr A.D.E. Rippon	c Miller b Vincett	60	b Cox	8
Mr J.C.W. MacBryan	lbw b Cox	18	b Cox	0
E. Robson	b Cox	14	b Roberts	11
L. C. Braund	b Roberts	3	b Roberts	11
Mr J.D. Harcombe	c H.L. Wilson b Cox	0	run out	5
Mr P.P. Hope	c Tate b Vincett	48	c Stannard b Vincett	6
J.F. Bridges	c Miller b Vincett	34	st Miller b Vincett	14
Capt Amor	b Cox	14	c Cox b Tate	13
*Mr J.C. White	b Cox	12	not out	11
#H. Chidgey	not out	1	c Vincett b Cox	10
Extras	(b8, lb4, w1)	13	(b5, w1)	6
TOTAL		243		103

Bowling	O	M	R	W	O	M	R	W
Roberts	17	4	51	1	16	1	40	2
Vincett	31	4	69	3	9	0	20	2
Stannard	8	0	27	1				
Tate	12	3	32	0	6	1	11	1
Cox	15.4	4	51	5	18.4	6	26	4

SUSSEX

*Mr H.L. Wilson	b Bridges	56	not out	42
Mr A.K. Wilson	c Braund b Bridges	4	c Braund b Robson	4
Mr T.E. Bourdillon	b Bridges	21	c Bridges b Robson	7
Mr A.C. Somerset	b Robson	33	c Braund b Robson	0
# Mr R.A.T. Miller	b Bridges	2	c Bridges b White	0
Mr J.H. Vincett	b Bridges	14	b Bridges	6
H.E. Roberts	b Robson	5	b A.D.E. Rippon	28
M.W. Tate	c Braund b Robson	69	c Chidgey b Bridges	11
G.A. Stannard	b A.D.E. Rippon	3	c MacBryan b A.D.E. Rippon	0
G. Cox	not out	24	b Bridges	0
Mr H.J. Heygate	b White	0	absent	
Extras	(b5, lb6)	11	(b1, lb 5)	6
TOTAL		242		104

Bowling	O	M	R	W	O	M	R	W
White	18.4	1	76	1	3.3	0	14	1
Robson	15	3	49	3	14	2	51	3
Bridges	22	4	84	5	12	2	32	3
A.D.E. Rippon	9	2	22	1	2	1	1	2

Umpires: F.G. Roberts and A.E. Street

Match Tied

SUSSEX *v.* HAMPSHIRE

6, 8 and 9 May 1922 County Championship
Southampton

Arthur Gilligan's first match as Sussex captain produced a victory when the result might have been so very different. On a pleasant Saturday morning at the Northlands Road ground in Southampton, he won the toss and elected to bat. For much of its history, Sussex has produced strong batting sides, but these have often been let down by some far from incisive bowling. For a few years in the early 1920s, the opposite may well have been the case, Ted Bowley being the only class batsman in the side before the emergence of Duleepsinhji and Tommy Cook.

On this occasion, Sussex got off to a poor start, Bowley, Harold Gilligan and 'Tich' Cornford all going for ducks, and it was left to Maurice Tate and George Street to give the total a modest respectability. Hampshire fared even worse: Arthur Gilligan, low-armed but decidedly fast, came on as second change and demolished the home side, whose innings ended exactly 100 runs behind Sussex. By the close on the Saturday, Sussex's second innings stood at 62 for 2 wickets, a substantial lead in what was appearing to be a low-scoring match.

On the Monday morning, Tate and Harold Gilligan both took their scores into the 70s and, with the skipper himself weighing in with a useful 42, the visitors' innings closed at 218 – not a great performance, but a lead of 318. To win, Hampshire would have to make by far the highest score of the match and, when George Brown was quickly dismissed, it looked as though Sussex were in for an easy victory. Hampshire, however, were not to be brushed aside so easily. Alec Kennedy and Alec Bowell came together in a second-wicket partnership of 151 and, when Kennedy was dismissed, Bowell was joined by Phil Mead, certainly Hampshire's greatest batsman of the inter-war years. By the close on Monday evening, these three batsmen had swung the game back firmly to Hampshire as they needed a mere 63 runs for victory with 8 wickets left.

In these days, when amateurs and professionals were different sorts of cricketers, it was not unheard of for the amateurs from both sides to use the same dressing-room. The days of calculated animosity between sides were still in the distant future and, on the Tuesday morning before play began, Gilligan and the Hampshire captain, Lionel Tennyson, discussed the match. Tennyson believed that the result was not a foregone conclusion and confided his concerns about his side's middle-order batting.

When Tennyson came in to bat, George Cox, who firmly believed that the Hampshire skipper was his personal rabbit, came up to his captain and said: 'I think I may well shift him if you will let me have a go.' Sure enough, Tennyson was lbw in the next over. How right he had been! 256 for 2 had become 295 for 9 and, although the last pair added another 14, Sussex finally ran out winners by a slim margin of 10 runs.

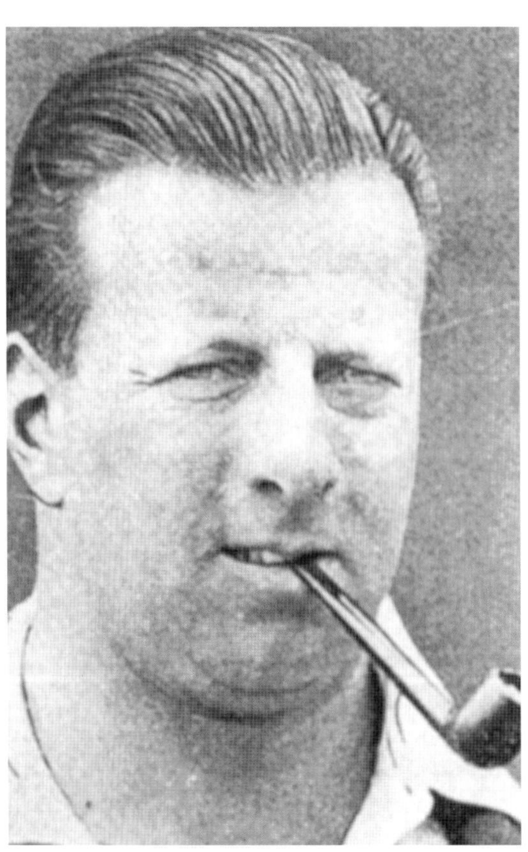

The Honourable Lionel Tennyson, Hampshire's captain.

Sussex won the toss and elected to bat

SUSSEX				
E.H. Bowley	b Kennedy	0	c Mead b Kennedy	0
M.W. Tate	b Kennedy	31	b Kennedy	71
Mr A.H.H. Gilligan	c Fry b Remnant	0	b Kennedy	74
#G. Street	not out	71	lbw b Kennedy	5
W. Cornford	run out	0	c Brown b Remnant	11
Lt Col A.C. Watson	c Brown b Remnant	18	b Newman	3
H.E. Roberts	b Kennedy	2	b Kennedy	1
*Mr A.E.R. Gilligan	c Bowell b Boyes	16	b Kennedy	42
G. Cox	b Newman	0	st Livsey b Newman	6
G. Stannard	b Newman	11	lbw b Kennedy	2
Mr A.A. Saunders	c Newman b Tennyson	14	not out	0
Extras	(b5, lb5)	10	(b1, lb2)	3
TOTAL		173		218

Bowling	O	M	R	W	O	M	R	W
Kennedy	24	6	55	3	22.1	3	71	7
Newman	20	6	66	2	19	1	70	2
Remnant	18	8	25	2	9	1	38	1
Boyes	7	1	16	1	2	0	13	0
Tennyson	1	0	1	1	2	0	9	0
Brown					4	1	14	0

HAMPSHIRE				
A. Kennedy	lbw b Roberts	8	b Cox	70
A. Bowell	b Roberts	0	run out	140
G. Brown	b Cox	9	st Street b Tate	5
C.P. Mead	b A. Gilligan	8	c Saunders b A.Gilligan	50
*Hon L.H. Tennyson	c and b Bowley	30	lbw b Cox	2
Mr S. Fry	b A. Gilligan	0	b Cox	0
J. Newman	c Street b A. Gilligan	3	b Cox	3
Mr A.E.L. Hill	b A. Gilligan	4	b Roberts	7
#W.H. Livsey	b A. Gilligan	0	b Roberts	0
G.S. Boyes	b A. Gilligan	0	not out	4
E.R. Remnant	not out	6	c Roberts b A. Gilligan	10
Extras	(b1, lb4)	5	(b11, lb4, w1, nb1)	17
TOTAL		73		308

Bowling	O	M	R	W	O	M	R	W
Roberts	7	2	22	2	13	4	35	2
Tate	4	3	5	0	14	3	39	1
Cox	8	2	18	1	40	9	90	4
A.E.R. Gilligan	8	3	18	6	23.2	2	66	2
Bowley	2	0	5	1	11	0	35	0
A.H.H. Gilligan					3	0	12	0
Stannard					6	0	14	0

Umpires: T. Flowers and J.H. Board

Sussex won by 10 runs

SUSSEX v. MIDDLESEX

7 and 9 June 1924 — County Championship
Lord's

The Whitsun matches at Lord's between Sussex and Middlesex were once a permanent feature of the cricketing calendar, but the new style of fixture list has tended to override such traditions. The 1924 match – a low-scoring match in itself – ended in disaster for the home team when Sussex ran out winners by the relatively large margin of 194 runs.

On the Saturday morning, despite the rather threatening weather, almost 10,000 spectators went through the turnstiles at 1s per head, and on the Bank Holiday Monday, the official number attending came to 15,731. Lord's had been drenched by repeated downpours the previous week, but Harry White and his Lord's groundstaff had worked miracles in producing the wicket. For all that, however, runs were hard to come by and, in the face of the bowling of Nigel Haig and Greville Stevens, Sussex reached a meagre 156, in the course of which Harold Gilligan, 'endeavouring to place Durston to leg', to quote the *Brighton Evening Argus* reporter, 'was given out for obstruction'. What was meant, of course, was that he was lbw! Gilligan was always the perfect gentleman and did not obstruct fielders! Sussex's total was matched by an even less distinguished 104 from Middlesex, where Maurice Tate, now very much at the height of his powers, had the home side in real difficulty with 7 for 39. But for Gubby Allen's hard-fought 43, they would almost certainly have not reached three figures. The absence through a finger injury of 'Young Jack' Hearne, of course, did not aid their cause.

In the second innings, with openers Harold Gilligan and Ted Bowley giving them a fair start, Sussex batted with somewhat greater resolution, although only Maurice Tate on either side reached a half-century. Sussex's 183 was probably a better score than it looked on paper because the pitch was now showing signs of damage, and Middlesex's target of 236 was, in fact, a tall order. Arthur Gilligan, the Sussex skipper, was, however, in irresistible form and, backed by Tate at the other end, shot the hosts out for 41 by half-past five on the Monday afternoon, with only 'Patsy' Hendren on the home side offering any serious resistance. Except for the 5 overs bowled by George Cox in Middlesex's first innings, Gilligan and Tate bowled unchanged throughout the match. Sussex had won at Lord's for the first time since the First World War, but those who had hoped to watch cricket on the Tuesday were sadly disappointed.

1924 was a marvellous year for Tate and Gilligan. Not only did the former head Sussex's batting and bowling in the Championship with 1,095 runs and 139 wickets, but together they bowled South Africa out for 30 in the First Test at Edgbaston a week after they had so comprehensively demolished Middlesex.

Maurice Tate.

Arthur Gilligan.

This card does not necessarily include the fall of the last wicket.

2d. Lord's  Ground

MIDDLESEX v. SUSSEX.

SATURDAY & MONDAY, JUNE 7, 9, 1924. (3-day Match.)

SUSSEX.	First Innings.		Second Innings.	
1 A. H. H. Gilligan	l b w, b Durston	11	c Lee, b Haig	31
2 Bowley	c and b Kidd	16	b Haig	21
3 Cox	b Stevens	9	b Haig	7
4 Cook	b Kidd	0	b Stevens	1
5 Tate	b Stevens	11	c Crutchley, b Stevens	51
† 6 A. E. R. Gilligan	b Haig	35	b Haig	18
7 A. J. Holmes	not out	25	b Stevens	0
8 Parks	l b w, b Stevens	1	b Haig	5
9 Wensley	b Haig	1	b Haig	4
10 Colonel A. C. Watson	c Allen, b Haig	23	b Stevens	2
*11 Cornford	b Stevens	5	not out	13
	B 15, l-b 3, w , n-b 1	19	B 20, l-b 7, w , n-b 3,	30
	Total	156	Total	183

FALL OF THE WICKETS.

1-12	2-37	3-38	4-41	5-85	6-91	7-96	8-101	9-147	10-156
1-46	2-55	3-61	4-64	5-123	6-143	7-151	8-151	9-156	10-183

ANALYSIS OF BOWLING.

Name.	1st Innings O.	M.	R.	W.	Wd.	N-b.	2nd Innings O.	M.	R.	W.	Wd.	N-b
Haig	21	7	45	3	...	...	24.4	6	79	6	...	...
Durston	11	2	21	1	...	1	2	0	9	0	...	2
Kidd	8	2	23	2	...	...	...	...	...	...	...	...
Stevens	17.1	3	48	4	...	...	20	3	50	4	...	1
Allen	...	...	...	...	...	...	1	0	13	0	...	...
Lee	...	...	...	...	...	...	1	0	2	0	...	...
...	...	...	...	...	...	...	...	...	...	...	...	...

MIDDLESEX.	First Innings.		Second Innings.	
1 H. L. Dales	c Tate, b Cox	8	b A. E. R. Gilligan	0
2 Lee, H. W.	l b w, b A. E. R. Gilligan	2	b A. E. R. Gilligan	5
3 G. T. S. Stevens	b Tate	6	l b w, b A. E. R. Gilligan	3
4 Hendren, E.	b A. E. R. Gilligan	15	c Bowley, b A.E.Gilligan	17
5 E. L. Kidd	b Tate	6	c Cox, b Tate	1
† 6 F. T. Mann	b Tate	6	c and b A. E. R. Gilligan	0
7 G. E. V. Crutchley	b Tate	3	c A. H. Gilligan, b Tate	2
8 N. Haig	b Tate	0	c Holmes, b A.E.Gilligan	3
9 G. O. Allen	not out	43	l b w, b A. E. R. Gilligan	0
*10 Murrell	b Tate	2	not out	5
11 Durston	c Wensley, b Tate	5	b A. E. R. Gilligan	2
	B 4, l-b 4, w , n-b ,	8	B 2, l-b 1, w , n-b ,	3
	Total	104	Total	41

FALL OF THE WICKETS.

1-2	2-17	3-25	4-40	5-42	6-45	7-45	8-76	9-80	10-104
1-1	2-1	3-12	4-13	5-24	6-28	7-31	8-31	9-39	10-41

ANALYSIS OF BOWLING.

Name.	1st Innings O.	M.	R.	W.	Wd.	N-b.	2nd Innings O.	M.	R.	W.	Wd.	N-b
A. E. R. Gilligan	24	9	46	2	...	...	14	5	25	8	...	...
Tate	28.5	13	39	7	...	...	13	3	13	2	...	...
Cox	5	3	11	1	...	...	...	...	...	...	...	...
...	...	...	...	...	...	...	...	...	...	...	...	...
...	...	...	...	...	...	...	...	...	...	...	...	...
...	...	...	...	...	...	...	...	...	...	...	...	...
...	...	...	...	...	...	...	...	...	...	...	...	...
...	...	...	...	...	...	...	...	...	...	...	...	...

Umpires—Watts and Street. Scorers—Burton and Byrne.

Play commences 1st day at 12, 2nd and 3rd day at 11.

The figures on the Scoring Board show the Batsmen in.

Luncheon at 1.30. † Captain. * Wicket-keeper. Stumps drawn at 6.30

TEA INTERVAL—There will probably be a Tea Interval at **4.15-4.30** but it will depend on the state of the game.

SUSSEX *v.* WARWICKSHIRE

5, 7 and 8 June 1926 — County Championship
Horsham

'Off his own bat' would not be appropriate, but if ever a Sussex player defeated another county almost on his own, then the occasion would certainly be the County's victory over Warwickshire during the Horsham Cricket Week in 1926. In his fifty-third year, George Rubens Cox, playing on what he liked to describe as his 'home' ground (owing to its proximity to his native village of Warnham some three miles away), took 17 of the Warwickshire wickets to fall and led Sussex to a victory that at times was no foregone conclusion. The visitors batted first on the Saturday, and good innings by Len Bates and William Quaife, who might have enjoyed a career with Sussex had not winter employment prospects been better in Birmingham than in Brighton, brought them a solid, but not outstanding total of 257. Sussex were without the services of both Arthur Gilligan and Maurice Tate, but Cox, from the railway end, bowled his slow left-arm spin with such control that, in the course of 38.4 overs, he sent back eight Warwickshire batsmen at a cost of 7 runs each.

Sussex did not bat with much aplomb. Although Jim Parks nearly reached his half-century, the normally wholly reliable Ted Bowley and the County's middle-order all failed, and it was left to the amateurs 'Jack' Holmes, who batted for two and a half hours, and Harold Gilligan to give the total some respectability and secure a modest first-innings lead of 4 runs. When Warwickshire went in again, Cox proved just as effective as he had done in their first innings. As John Marshall, the Sussex cricket historian, described it: 'Cox had the batsmen shuffling from unease to helplessness, getting an edge on it – or not even an edge at all – baffled and bewildered.' Although John Parsons scrambled to a half-century, the visiting batsmen could make nothing of Cox and he ended with nine scalps. In taking 17 of the 20 Warwickshire wickets, he bowled himself into the record books and, to the present day, only Jim Laker's 19 wickets against Australia in 1956 has bettered 17 wickets in a match, although a fair number share the honour with Cox. A total of 9 batsmen were bowled, 4 were dismissed by 'Tich' Cornford and 4 were caught in the field in the course of 36.5 overs at a cost of 50 runs.

The final day was interrupted by rain and Sussex found themselves with three hours to score the 174 needed for victory. Bowley and Bert Wensley overcame their first-innings failures and the County ran out winners by 5 wickets in the last over. Among the spectators at this match was George Cox junior, who treasured for many a year the ball with which his father had triumphed so remarkably. Cox did not stop at this point and played another full season for the County in 1927. He retired only after the 1928 season to enter the world of coaching.

George Cox senior (right) with Alan Saunders (centre) and Reginald Hollingdale.

Play first day 12 noon to 6.45. Second day 11.15 to 6.45. Third day 11.15 to 5.30.

For Commercial & Private Printing & Stationery go to Fred Holmes, The Printer, 17, North St., Horsham.

TWOPENCE. Horsham Cricket Week.

OFFICIAL SCORE, 1926.

Saturday, Monday and Tuesday, June 5th, 7th & 8th.

SUSSEX V. WARWICKSHIRE.

WARWICKSHIRE.	First Innings.		Second Innings.	
1 Parsons	b Bowley	20	b Cox	50
2 R. E. Wyatt	c Watson, b Cox	33	c Cornford, b Cox	35
3 Bates	b Cox	77	c Wensley, b Cox	30
4 Quaife	b Cox	43	c Bowley, b Cox	1
5 Santall	c Cook, b Langridge	5	st Cornford, b Cox	7
6 N. E. Partridge	b Cox	12	b Wensley	3
7 Croom	c Bowley, b Cox	15	not out	23
8 Kilner	st Cornford, b Cox	28	b Cox	0
9 Smart	st Cornford, b Cox	15	b Cox	23
10 Peare	b Cox	0	b Cox	0
11 Mayer	not out	2	b Cox	1
	Extras	7	Extras	4
Cox—8 wickets for 56.	Total	257	Cox—9 for 50. Total	177

1-48 2-60 3-171 4-176 5-192 6-199 7-220 8-240 9-240 10-257

1-72 2-91 3-99 4-104 5-121 6-123 7-136 8-175 9-177 10-177

SUSSEX.	First Innings.		Second Innings.	
1 Bowley	b Mayer	8	b Wyatt	53
2 Parks (J.)	c Bates, b Quaife	48	c Partridge, b Quaife	22
3 Wensley	b Santall	5	c Mayer, b Wyatt	40
4 Cook	c Wyatt, b Quaife	20	not out	9
5 Langridge	b Partridge	5		
6 A. J. Holmes	b Partridge	87	not out	8
7 Cox	c Bates, b Quaife	0		
8 A. H. Gilligan	c Partridge, b Parsons	20	run out	15
9 Col. A. C. Watson	b Partridge	11	run out	19
10 Parks (H.)	b Mayer	14		
11 Cornford	not out	12		
Quaife—3 wickets for 34.	Extras	31	Extras	8
Mayer—2 wickets for 15.	Total	261	Total	174

1-23 2-29 3-75 4-94 5-94 6-94 7-123 8-147 9-205 10-261

1-46 2-122 3-122 4-141 5-164 6- 7- 8- 9- 10-

Umpires: Young and Street. Scorers: Austin and Isaacs.

'Phone 190. Fred Holmes, The Printer, 17, North Street, Horsham. ☞ For High-Class Printing.

Luncheon, 1.30 to 2.15. Tea, 4.15. ☞ P.T.O.

SUSSEX *v.* KENT

10, 12 and 13 August 1929
Hastings

County Championship

Games between Kent and Sussex, especially in the 1920s, have rarely been 'grudge' matches, but the meeting between the two Counties at Hastings in 1929, almost certainly was. Even that most mannerly cricketer, K.S. Duleepsinhji, approached the game in a combative spirit. The reason stemmed from the previous encounter between Kent and Sussex at Maidstone in July. 'On a pitch watered too recently,' as *Wisden* so diplomatically reported it, 'batting first did not prove an advantage.' Although no captain can rig the toss, it is quite possible for a home side, who possesses the right sort of bowler, to provide a pitch which will help him. In Kent's case, this was 'Tich' Freeman and, by taking 13 wickets for 105 runs, he ensured that his side won by an innings before lunch on the second day.

Now, before a Saturday crowd of some 8,000 spectators at Hastings, the Sussex batsmen set off like an express train. Although Ted Bowley went early, Harold Gilligan, captaining the County in his brother's absence, and Duleep gained such mastery over the Kent bowlers that 121 runs came in fifty-five minutes and the score progressed from 52 to 104 in a quarter of an hour. Duleep, at his very best, scored his 115 in a hundred minutes, hitting Freeman for a six and scoring 14 fours, while Gilligan batted with refreshing vigour. After lunch, Jim Langridge and Bert Wensley (who made his 61 out of 97 in fifty minutes) continued to punish the Kent bowling, while towards the end of the County's innings, Romilly Holdsworth, a former Oxford blue who had not played the previous season, weighed in with 9 fours in his 69*. Claiming one Kent wicket before the close, Sussex had had a good day.

Sussex must have entered the second day brimming with confidence. When Woolley's hundred-minute innings came to an end and 5 wickets were down for 129 – and with Percy Chapman injured and unable to bat – the Sussex total must have seemed a long way off. So well did the Tonbridge schoolmaster, C.H. Knott, bat in partnership with Bill Ashdown and Charles Wright, however, that the visitors ended up only 30 runs short of the Sussex total; Maurice Tate, in the course of 41 overs, claiming 6 of their wickets for 136 runs. When Sussex went in again, it was, once more, all Duleepsinhji. By the time stumps were drawn, the County had reached 215 for 3 with the Indian master undefeated on 149.

Sussex at Hastings in 1930, from left to right, back row: W.L. Cornford, T.E.R. Cook, A.F. Wensley, R.L. Holdsworth, G.S. Grimston, R.A. Hollingdale, H.W. Parks, James Langridge. Front row: M.W. Tate, K.S. Duleepsinhji, A.H.H. Gilligan (captain), A.E.R. Gilligan, Sir Home Gordon, E.H. Bowley.

Sussex won the toss and elected to bat

SUSSEX

	1st innings		2nd innings	
E.H. Bowley	b Ashdown	3	lbw b Freeman	30
*Mr A.H.H. Gilligan	c Hardinge b Freeman	56	c Ashdown b Wright	4
Mr K.S. Duleepsinhji	c Bryan b Marriott	115	c sub b Freeman	246
T. Cook	c Wright b Freeman	7		
James Langridge	lbw b Woolley	80	c Ames b Ashdown	32
A.F. Wensley	c Marriott b Freeman	61	c Ashdown b Freeman	33
Mr R.L. Holdsworth	not out	69	lbw b Marriott	8
M.W. Tate	c Ames b Freeman	5	b Marriott	9
Mr G.S. Grimston	b Freeman	4	b Marriott	6
#W. Cornford	b Marriott	6	not out	6
R.A. Hollingdale	b Freeman	3		
Extras	(b13, lb5, nb1)	19	(b5, lb2)	7
TOTAL		428	(for 8 wkts dec.)	381

Bowling	O	M	R	W	O	M	R	W
Wright	16	2	61	0	18	1	73	1
Ashdown	15	5	62	1	19	1	97	1
Freeman	32.1	3	131	6	23	4	106	3
Marriott	17	1	91	2	15.2	2	69	3
Woolley	16	3	40	1	6	0	29	0
Hardinge	7	1	21	0				
Todd	2	0	3	0				

KENT

	1st innings		2nd innings	
H.T.W. Hardinge	b Tate	22	c Duleepsinhji b Tate	5
Mr J.L. Bryan	c Duleepsinhji b Tate	3	c Hollingdale b Tate	17
F.E. Woolley	c Hollingdale b Tate	58	c Duleepsinhji b Tate	4
#L.E.G. Ames	c Duleepsinhji b Cook	14	b Tate	118
W.H. Ashdown	c Cornford b Tate	63	b Tate	21
L.J. Todd	c Wensley b Hollingdale	6	c sub b Wensley	43
Mr C.H. Knott	not out	140	not out	26
C. Wright	c Duleepsinhji b Wensley	69	c Duleepsinhji b Tate	0
A.P. Freeman	b Tate	0	c Gilligan b Wensley	0
Mr C.S. Marriott	c Cornford b Tate	0	c Langridge b Tate	3
*Mr A.P.F. Chapman	absent hurt		absent hurt	
Extras	(b6, lb15, nb2)	23	(b5, lb1, nb1)	7
TOTAL		398		244

Bowling	O	M	R	W	O	M	R	W
Tate	41	5	136	6	23.3	6	58	7
Wensley	30	6	80	1	23	3	85	2
Cook	11	4	30	1				
Hollingdale	9	1	32	1	10	4	24	0
Langridge	8	3	36	0	5	0	34	0
Bowley	8	0	37	0	5	0	16	0
Grimston	9	1	24	0	2	0	20	0

Umpires: J.W. Day and J. Hardstaff

Sussex won by 167 runs

Romilly Holdsworth scored quickly.

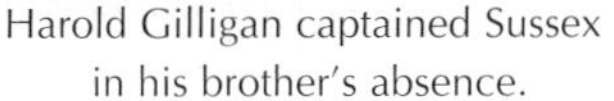

Harold Gilligan captained Sussex in his brother's absence.

Bert Wensley.

He had reached 50 in under an hour, had doubled his score in half an hour and reached his second hundred of the match with a glorious straight six off Woolley.

Tuesday morning saw the continuation of the glorious weather that had made the 1929 Hastings Festival as successful as any in its history. Duleep did not waste any time and added a further 97 in seventy minutes, before falling to a catch at long-on. His innings, which contained 5 sixes and 31 fours, had been full of handsome drives and shots on the leg-side and represented nearly 66 per cent of the runs off the bat in the Sussex total. Soon after 12.30 p.m., 166 runs having been added in ninety minutes, Gilligan was able to declare and set Kent the mighty total of 412 to win in three hours and forty minutes. A pair of early wickets before lunch and 2 more immediately afterwards – all 4 to Tate – left Kent reeling at 66 for 4, but Ames and Todd batted steadily and then increased their tempo, so that 128 runs were added for the fifth wicket in seventy-five minutes. After the tea interval, the new ball became due and Tate clean-bowled Ames. Together with Wensley, he soon polished off the Kent tail, leaving Sussex the winners by the clear margin of 167 runs. Tate did even better than in the first innings, bowling 23.3 overs and taking 7 Kent wickets for 58 runs.

For Duleep, this must have been some compensation for what he and the Sussex team had perceived as Kentish skulduggery at Maidstone, but he had also achieved some personal fame. He became only the fifth player in first-class cricket to score a hundred in one innings and two hundred in the other; one of the four who had preceded him was, of course, Sussex's C.B. Fry, who scored 125 and 229 against Surrey in 1900. The match in itself was also a winner: the aggregate of 1,451 runs for the loss of 36 wickets was, at the time, the second highest made in a County Championship match, bettered only by the Surrey versus Northamptonshire encounter of 1920, although these aggregates have subsequently been superseded.

SUSSEX *v.* NORTHAMPTONSHIRE

7, 8 and 9 May 1930 County Championship
Hove

The 1930 season saw Harold Gilligan succeed his brother as captain and Duleepsinhji ready to build on his performances of 1929. After having had a draw against Nottinghamshire, Sussex came to their second match of the season against Northamptonshire, who were led by the former Sussex player, Vallance Jupp. The pitch was soft when Ted Bowley and Jim Parks opened the County's innings on the Wednesday morning and, by the time the score had reached 30, both of them were back in the pavilion. Duleep, however, was in prime form, 'scoring all round the wicket with delightful ease' as the *Daily Telegraph* reporter noted, and supported in a third-wicket stand of 77 by Tommy Cook, he reached his half-century in little over an hour. By lunchtime, Sussex's poor start was being retrieved.

After the lunch interval, 'Nobby' Clark, the Northamptonshire left-arm pace bowler, caused the batsmen some difficulty and restrained Duleep for a time, but he was not to be tied down and reached his hundred out of 141 in just over two hours. His partnership of 75 in eighty minutes with James Langridge was ended when the left-hander was bowled at 182 and, when Harry Parks also went cheaply, the Northamptonshire bowling, which had never been loose, was beginning to re-assert itself. The Hove wicket, however, had by then dried out and was playing very easily, and Duleep moved to his double hundred, made out of 293, in just over four hours. He soon went past his previous highest score of 254*, made for Cambridge University in 1927, and, with Maurice Tate, he began to savage the visitors' tiring attack. The 285* made by Duleep's uncle, Ranjitsinhji, against Somerset in 1901 was left behind, and Duleep's triple hundred came up in five-and-a-quarter hours. In the meantime, Tate had been hitting furiously and reached his century in ninety-five minutes with 2 sixes and 10 fours. When Tate was out with the score at 490, he and Duleep had added 255 in only 105 minutes. Duleep's great innings, full of sparkling drives and glorious square-cuts and containing 1 six and 34 fours, came to an end just before the close, by which time Sussex were past the 500-mark.

After Harold Gilligan had declared, the Northamptonshire batsmen faced the uphill task of reaching 372 to avoid the follow-on. Against the medium-fast attack of Tate and Bert Wensley, and the slow-medium swingers of Jim Parks, they scrambled to 84 for 4 at lunchtime and the innings subsided during the afternoon to 187 all out. Their second innings began disastrously and, when the fifth wicket fell at 45, Tate had taken 4 wickets at a personal cost of 22 runs. Despite some spirited middle-order resistance, the Midlanders ended the day on 106 for 6 wickets and were overwhelmingly beaten after forty minutes on the next morning.

Duleepsinhji's remarkable 333 remains today the highest score ever made for the County and, in fact, the only triple hundred recorded by a Sussex player.

Duleep – Sussex's only triple centurion.

SUSSEX WON BY AN INNINGS AND 209 RUNS.

2d. SUSSEX COUNTY CRICKET GROUND, HOVE. 2d.

May 7, 8 & 9, 1930. SUSSEX v. NORTHANTS. Sussex won the Toss.

Play starts at 11.30 each day. Lunch at 1.30. Draw at 6.30.

SUSSEX	First Innings		Second Innings	
1 Bowley, E. H.	c Bellamy b Thomas	1		
2 Parks, J.	c Liddell b Thomas	9		
3 K. S. Duleepsinhji	st Bellamy b Matthews	333		
4 Parks, H.	b Clark	11		
5 Langridge, J.	b Cox	17		
6 Cook, T.	c Liddell b Clark	19		
7 Wensley, A.	not out	0		
8 A.H.H. Gilligan (Cpt.)	not out	8		
9 Tate, M. W.	b Partridge	111		
*10 Cornford, W.				
11 Hollingdale, R. A.				
	b. l.b. 6 w. n.b. 6	12	b. l.b. w. n.b.	
	(7 WKTS. DEC.) Total	521	Total—	

Runs at fall of wicket: 1-1 2-30 3-107 4-182 5-235 6-490 7-514 8- 9- 10-
1- 2- 3- 4- 5- 6- 7- 8- 9- 10-

Bowling Analysis.	o.	m.	r.	w.	wd.	n.b.	o.	m.	r.	w.	wd.	n.b.
Clark	27	1	75	2								
Thomas	29	11	69	2								
Partridge	12	0	80	1								
Matthews	22	2	101	1								
Jupp	20	3	92	0								
Cox	11	2	[illegible]	1								
Liddell	2	0	16	0								
Timms	3	0	26	0								

NORTHANTS	First Innings		Second Innings	
1 Woolley, C.	b Wensley	18	c Duleep b Wensley	4
2 Bakewell, A.	lbw b J. Parks	12	b Tate	7
3 Timms, J. E.	c J. Parks b Langridge	19	lbw b Tate	20
4 V. C. W. Jupp (Cpt.)	c Duleep b Wensley	0	lbw b Tate	11
5 Matthews, A.	lbw b J. Parks	13	c Duleep b Tate	0
*6 Bellamy, B.	b Wensley	21	c Cornford b Tate	35
7 Liddell, A.	c Gilligan b Bowley	18	c Cook b Tate	28
8 Cox, A.	lbw b Tate	40	c Cornford b Cook	4
9 Thomas, A.	lbw b Wensley	29	b Hollingdale	11
10 Partridge, R.	not out	3	b Tate	2
11 Clark, E.	b Tate	1	not out	0
	b. 9 l.b. 4 w. n.b.	13	b. 2 l.b. 1 w. n.b.	3
	Total—	187	Total	125

Runs at fall of wicket: 1-28 2-28 3-32 4-70 5-84 6-102 7-113 8-175 9-183 10-187
1-13 2-13 3-44 4-45 5-45 6-97 7-106 8-119 9-124 10-125

Bowling Analysis.	o.	m.	r.	w.	wd.	n.b.	o.	m.	r.	w.	wd.	n.b.
Tate	9.5	1	18	2			20.2	3	45	7		
Wensley	28	10	45	4			14	5	41	1		
J. Parks	22	11	37	2			[illegible]	[illegible]	[illegible]	0		
Langridge	14	7	21	1			[illegible]	[illegible]	[illegible]	1		
Hollingdale	10	2	21	0			8	[illegible]	14	1		

* Wicket Keeper. Umpires—Toone & Chester Scorers—E. Killick & L. Bullimer

Next Match on this Ground—May 24, 26, 27, SUSSEX v. SOMERSET.

Printed on the Ground by H. CROWHURST, Printer to the S.C.C.C., 50-1-2, Market Street, Brighton.

SUSSEX *v.* MIDDLESEX

5, 7 and 8 August 1933
Hove

County Championship

In August 1933, Sussex were experiencing one of the best periods of sustained successful cricket in their history. Fourth in the County Championship in 1931 and second the following season, Sussex were scarcely missing the potent batting of Duleepsinhji whose ill health had caused his premature retirement from the game. In 1933, they came to the Bank Holiday fixture with Middlesex with 14 wins from 27 matches under their belt.

The Saturday crowd at Hove witnessed a remarkable day's cricket when Ted Bowley and John Langridge batted for almost the whole day to put on 490 for the first wicket. At a stroke, this stand broke two County records: it went past the previous highest first-wicket stand of 368, which Bowley (280*) had established with Jim Parks senior (110) against Gloucestershire in 1929, and at the same time it eclipsed the highest stand for any wicket in the County's history. This, too, had involved Bowley when he (228) and Maurice Tate (203) had flayed the Northamptonshire attack at Hove in 1921 to the tune of 385. The fact that Bowley was now in his forty-fourth year and in his last full season with Sussex made the event perhaps all the more poignant.

From the outset, Bowley and Langridge mastered the Middlesex bowling with ease, and the former reached 50 out of 82 in an hour. Had he not missed a fair amount of the strike at a critical stage, he might well have reached his hundred before lunch. As it was, he was successful a quarter of an hour after lunch and, by the time the umpires took the players off for tea with the score on 355, he had come to his double ton. Although the Middlesex bowlers had performed manfully and caused some occasional discomfort to both players, the batsman-friendly Hove wicket and the fast outfield meant that Middlesex remained constantly on the back foot. After five hours' play, the 400 went up and gradually the stand edged towards 500. The thought must have emerged in the minds of the spectators – and perhaps the batsmen – that the world-record opening stand of 555, established by Herbert Sutcliffe and Percy Holmes of Yorkshire in the

The Hove scoreboard showing the huge opening stand.

John Langridge.

SUSSEX WON BY AN INNINGS AND 65 RUNS

2d. SUSSEX COUNTY CRICKET GROUND, HOVE. 2d.

Aug 5, 7, 8, 1933. SUSSEX v. MIDDLESEX. Sussex won toss.

Hours of Play—1st day, 11.30 to 7.0. 2nd : 11.0 to 7.0. 3rd : 11.0 to 4.0 or 4.30
Lunch at 1.30. Tea 4.15.

SUSSEX	First Innings		Second Innings	
1 Bowley, E. H.	c Hulme b Lee	283		
2 Langridge, John	lbw b Sims	195		
3 Parks, J.	c Enthoven b Sims	5		
4 Cook, T.	not out	2		
5 Langridge, James	not out	10		
6 Parks, H.				
7 R. S. G. Scott (Capt.)				
8 Wensley, A.				
9 Tate, M. W.				
*10 Cornford, W.				
11 Cornford, J.				
	b. 6 l.b. 11 w. n.b.	17	b. l.b. w. n.b.	
	(3 wkts dec) Total—	512	Total—	

Runs at fall of wicket	1-	2-	3-	4-	5-	6-	7-	8-	9-	10-
	1-490	2-500	3-502	4-	5-	6-	7-	8-	9-	10-
	1-	2-	3-	4-	5-	6-	7-	8-	9-	10-

Bowling Analysis	o.	m.	r.	w.	wd.	n.b.	o.	m.	r.	w.	wd.	n.b.
Nevinson	25	4	84	0								
Hulme	8	1	33	0								
Sims	31	2	122	2								
Enthoven	13	2	42	0								
Hearne	10	0	53	0								
Haig	20	1	63	0								
Allen	7	1	8	0								
Lee	27	2	90	1								

MIDDLESEX	First Innings		Second Innings	
1 Lee, H.	b Tate	10	b Tate	0
*2 Price, F.	c John Langridge b J. Parks	15	b Tate	4
3 Hearne, J. W.	lbw b Wensley	12	lbw b Tate	0
4 Hendren, E.	b Wensley	79	b J. Cornford	17
5 G. O. Allen	c W. Cornford b Tate	23	b Jas Langridge	80
6 Hulme, J.	c W. Cornford b Jas Langridge	19	c J. Cornford b Tate	35
7 H. J. Enthoven	lbw b Jas Langridge	8	c W. Cornford b Jas Langridge	4
8 N. Haig, (Capt.)	c Cook b Jas Langridge	41	b Jas Langridge	2
9 Sims, J. M.	not out	36	st W. Cornford b Jas Langridge	0
10 Watkins, W. R.	run out	25	c Scott b Jas Langridge	1
11 J. H. Nevinson	b Tate	0	not out	0
	b. 8 l.b. 12 w. n.b. 2	22	b. l.b. 14 w. n.b.	14
	Total—	290	Total—	157

Runs at fall of wicket	1-	2-	3-	4-	5-	6-	7-	8-	9-	10-
	1-26	2-36	3-54	4-110	5-163	6-177	7-183	8-226	9-290	10-290
	1-0	2-0	3-5	4-45	5-110	6-124	7-126	8-130	9-148	10-157

Bowling Analysis.	o.	m.	r.	w.	wd.	n.b.	o	m.	r.	w.	wd.	n.b.
Tate	28	10	41	3			15	5	20	4		
J. Cornford	20	4	61	0			16	6	34	1		
J. Parks	10	1	25	1								
Jas Langridge	30	10	68	3			20.3	7	33	5		
Wensley	26	6	53	2			17	2	42	0		
Bowley	5	0	20	0			2	0	14	0		

*Wicket Keeper. Umpires – Reeves & Baldwin Scorers—E. Killick & H. Murrell

Next Match on this Ground—August 16, 17, 18, SUSSEX v. GLAMORGAN

Printed on the Ground by H. CROWHURST Printer to the S.C.C.C., 50-1-2, Market Street, Brighton.

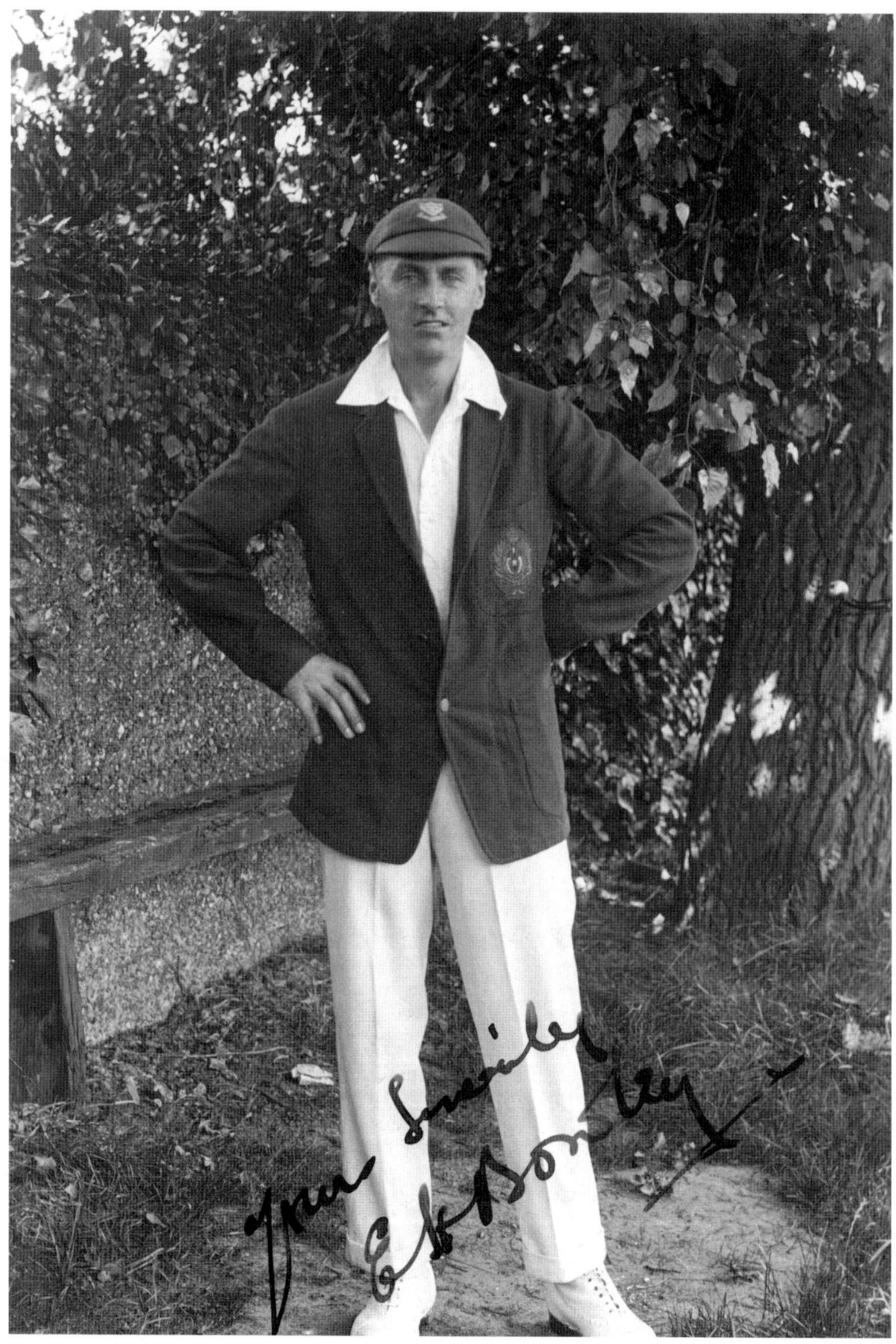

Ted Bowley.

Robert Scott, Sussex captain.

1932 season, might be about to be broken. But it was not to be.

With the score on 490, the spin of Jim Sims trapped Langridge lbw just 5 runs short of his double hundred. There was some irony, however, in his dismissal. It had been agreed, unusually, to play until 7.00 p.m. and his dismissal took place at 6.33 p.m., three minutes after the normal time of closure. Had this not occurred, it is possible that the pair might have resumed afresh on Monday morning with the record in sight. As things were, 2 more wickets went down and, when stumps were drawn, the Sussex score stood at 512 for 3 wickets. One of the wickets was Bowley's, his 283, scored in little more than six hours, containing 2 sixes, 1 five and 23 fours.

Robert Scott declared first thing on Monday morning, and it proved a disappointing day for the Middlesex team. Maurice Tate and Jim Parks soon disposed of their openers and, although 'Patsy' Hendren and Nigel Haig batted well, Middlesex could muster no more than 290 and were invited to follow-on. Their second innings started disastrously, Tate bowling Harry Lee with the second ball of the innings and sending back Hearne first ball. With only 5 on the board, Fred Price became Tate's third victim – his analysis at this stage being 3 wickets for 1 run. A finish on the second day seemed a real possibility, but Hendren and 'Gubby' Allen were not so easily overcome, and the visitors ended the day on 92 for 4 wickets.

Play on Tuesday morning, however, lasted no more than ninety minutes. Tate took one more wicket, but it was left to the slow left-arm spin of James Langridge to bring resistance to an end, despite a patient innings by Allen. One interesting vignette is the story of the member who congratulated John Langridge on his innings as he went out to field on the second morning, but added: 'You were a bit slow, John.' It was true that he was the best part of one hundred runs behind his partner, but barely two weeks later against Glamorgan, Langridge swept everything before him and reached 250* in seven hours of glorious batting.

SUSSEX *v.* NOTTINGHAMSHIRE

27, 29 and 30 June 1936 County Championship
Hove

Enmity, especially amongst those who have the longest pedigrees in the Championship, is, thankfully, a rare occurrence. The County's match with Nottinghamshire in 1936, however, nearly brought this condition of amity to an abrupt end. Bert Wensley, in his last season, had selected the Nottinghamshire match for his benefit, so it was sad that it ended in controversy. On the opening Saturday morning, the whole Nottinghamshire side, now leading the County Championship, had trooped into the Sussex dressing-room to wish Wensley luck with his benefit. Although Maurice Tate was not among the wicket-takers, Jim Cornford (whom many fancied at the time as another Maurice), Jim Hammond and Jim Parks, with slow-medium swingers, shot the visitors out for 74. Although Sussex lost both openers cheaply and the middle order failed to come up to scratch, Alan Melville, in his last season with the County, and his successor as captain, 'Jack' Holmes, pulled the innings together. Melville, suffering from an injured leg but playing with his usual elegance and power, was joined by Holmes in a partnership of 91 for the sixth wicket, which formed the core of the Sussex innings. Holmes went on to his hundred and reached what was then his highest score, as the County gained a substantial first-innings lead of 253 before declaring.

When Nottinghamshire batted for a second time, Walter Keeton and Willis Walker added 108 for the second wicket and George Gunn also batted well, but Tate and Parks were as economical as ever, and Cornford and Hammond bowled so effectively that the visitors were only 8 runs in credit when they were all out. With five minutes of the extra half-hour of time remaining, Sussex went in, seeking 9 runs for victory. The first over yielded 7 runs and then it started to drizzle. George Heane, the Nottinghamshire captain, appealed to the umpires and his team was allowed to leave the field. When taxed by Sussex secretary, W.L. Knowles, umpire Jack Newman later explained: 'Mr Heane told me he did not want to keep his men out in the rain. I told him there was time for another over, but he insisted and we left the field.'

Inevitably, this precipitate and unsporting action led to recriminations that were widely publicised at the time. Sussex threatened, perhaps quite reasonably, to cancel fixtures with the Midland club, but in the end a reply was received from Nottinghamshire which gave the County 'complete satisfaction.' It was pleasant that a long and flourishing friendship was not impaired, but how the ECB might have reacted nowadays certainly gives pause for thought. One imagines, perhaps, the docking of points from Nottinghamshire, which would have been a wholly justifiable action. Bert Wensley realised £1,030 (a reasonable sum in 1936) for his benefit, but his form was now deserting him. He played in only 15 Championship matches, making fewer than 250 runs and taking only 15 wickets at 49 runs each, and his decision to retire was undoubtedly correct.

George Heane, Nottinghamshire captain, who wanted to keep his players out of the rain.

DRAWN

This Card does not necessarily include the fall of the last wicket.

2d. SUSSEX COUNTY CRICKET GROUND, HOVE 2d.

June 27, 29, 30, 1936. SUSSEX v. NOTTS. Notts won toss

Hours of Play: 1st day, 11.30 to 6.30 2nd, 11.30 to 6.30. 3rd, 11.30 to 6 or 6.30
Lunch at 1.30. Tea at 4.15.

SUSSEX	First Innings		Second Innings	
1 Langridge, John	c Voce b Butler	21		
2 Parks, J.	b Butler	9	not out	2
3 A. Melville	b Voce	125		
4 Cook, T.	c Lilley b Butler	11	not out	0
5 Hammond, H. E.	lbw b Butler	0		
6 Parks, H.	run out	7		
7 A J. Holmes (Capt.)	c Staples b Heane	107		
8 Wensley, A.	c Harris b Heane	28		
9 Tate, M. W.	b Voce	9		
*10 Cornford, W	not out	2		
11 Cornford, J.				
	b. 4 l.b. 3 w. 1 n.b.	8	b 4 l.b 1 w. n.b	5
	(9 wkts dec) Total –	327	(no wkt) Total	7

Runs at fall of wicket
1-13 2-64 3-114 4-114 5-131 6-222 7-298 8-313 9-327 10-
1- 2- 3- 4- 5- 6- 7- 8- 9- 10-

Bowling Analysis	o.	m.	r.	w.	wd.	n.b	o.	m.	r.	w.	wd.	n.b
Voce	34	6	66	2			1	0	2	0		
Butler	26	5	69	4								
Woodhead	17	2	42	0								
Staples	17	2	45	0								
Knowles	6	0	25	0								
Heane	14.4	0	72	2								

NOTTS.	First Innings		Second Innings	
1 Keeton, W.	c C'nford, W. b C'nford, J.	7	lbw b Tate	77
2 Harris C.	l.b.w. b Cornford, J	5	c Holmes b J. Parks	17
3 Walker, W.	l.b.w. (N) b Cornford, J	0	c W. Cornford b Hammond	71
4 Gunn. G.	c & b J. Parks	34	c & b J. Cornford	47
5 Staples, A.	c Holmes b Hammond	12	b Tate	0
6 Knowles, J.	c C'nford, W b C'nford, J.	0	c John Langridge b J. Cornford	1
7 G. F. Heane (Capt)	c Hammond b J. Parks	2	lbw b J. Cornford	9
*8 Lilley, B.	c Hammond b J. Parks	6	c Hammond b J. Cornford	5
9 Voce, W.	c Holmes b Hammond	0	not out	18
10 Woodhead F.	c H. Parks b Hammond	0	c John Langridge b Hammond	0
11 Butler, S.	not out	4	b Hammond	0
	b. 3 l.b. 1 w. n.b	4	b 15 l.b. 1 w. n.b.	16
	Total —	74	Total –	261

Runs at fall of wicket
1-12 2-12 3-27 4-27 5-60 6-62 7-62 8-63 9-63 10-74
1-42 2-150 3-189 4-206 5-219 6-228 7-233 8-246 9-259 10-261

Bowling Analysis.	o.	m.	r.	w.	wd.	n.b.	o	m.	r.	w.	wd.	n.b
Tate	10	5	13	0			45	19	73	2		
J. Cornford	11	3	31	4			32	8	70	4		
Hammond	8	2	16	3			22.3	6	55	3		
J. Parks	6.4	3	10	3			29	11	43	1		
Wensley							2	1	4	0		

*Wicket Keeper Umpires—Woolley & Newman Scorers – E. Killick & J. Carlin

Next Match on this Ground—July 8, 9, 10, SUSSEX v LANCASHIRE

Printed on the Ground by H. CROWHURST, Printer to the S.C.C.C., 10-1-2, Market Street, Brighton

Sussex v. Australians

27, 29 and 30 August 1938 Tourist Match
Hove

Jessop and Alletson before him and Smith after him all played magnificent innings, but many assert that the greatest piece of hitting ever at Hove was Hugh Bartlett's 157 against the Australians in 1938. It certainly was not the fastest, but it could easily be seen as the greatest in that it was made not against a County attack, but against the strength of the Australian Tourists, a not markedly changed side from the one that had played in the Oval Test match. What is more, the Australians were, at one stage, in real danger of defeat.

The Australians batted first and made a sound 336, with Lindsay Hassett and Bill Brown top-scoring. Sussex made a solid, but not spectacular start to their innings and, when John Langridge and Harry Parks had been dismissed, Bartlett joined fellow amateur, Bob Stainton, and began his innings relatively quietly. When Stainton was dismissed, Bartlett was joined by Jim Langridge and the fireworks started. Together they added 195 for the fourth wicket, as Bartlett reached his 50 in half an hour and his hundred in fifty-seven minutes, winning in the process the Lawrence Trophy for 1938. One over of Frank Ward's leg-spin disappeared for 21 runs, and altogether he struck 18 fours and 6 sixes, one of which landed on the patch of grass in front of the tavern beside the main gates. Jim Langridge, at the time, reckoned that he had never seen an innings like it and being, of course, the consummate professional that he always was, played his part in the partnership. He saw to it that Bartlett had as large a share of the strike as possible, and sprinted between wickets to save seconds as his partner raced towards his hundred. Sussex passed the Australians' total with only 4 wickets down and, when Bartlett's two-hour innings came to an end and Jim Langridge was also dismissed, George Cox saw to it that the County had finally a lead of 117.

In the Australians' second innings, 'Jack' Badcock, Charlie Walker and Lindsay Hassett were all suffering from minor injuries, but, unsurprisingly, the walking wounded, together with Sidney Barnes and Ben Barnett, all batted doggedly and another total of just 300 was posted. The County were left a bare fifty minutes to score 184 and that was too much, even for Hugh Bartlett.

Seen in many quarters as the most attractive left-hander since Frank Woolley, Bartlett was considered unfortunate not to receive Test match honours in 1938, especially as in July of the same year he had made 175* for the Gentlemen against the Players at Lord's in less than three hours. He was selected for the MCC tour to South Africa in the winter of 1938/39, but once again did not reach the Test match side. After the Second World War, he played a further four seasons for Sussex, but never regained his pre-war form.

Hugh Bartlett scored his hundred in 57 minutes.

DRAWN

Autograph Hunting Is Forbidden, Offenders are liable to be turned out of the Ground
The Australians and Sussex XI. have been asked not to give any Autographs.

This Card does not necessarily include the fall of the last wicket.

2d. SUSSEX COUNTY CRICKET GROUND, HOVE, 2d.

Aug. 27, 29, 30, 1938. SUSSEX v. AUSTRALIANS. Australians won toss

Hours of Play: 1st day, 11.30 to 6.30 2nd, 11.30 to 6.30 3rd, 11.30 to 5.30
Lunch at 1.30. Tea at 4.15.

SUSSEX.	First Innings		Second Innings	
1 Langridge, John	st Walker b Ward	32	ST. BARNETT b WARD	13
2 R. G. Stainton	lbw b Ward	58	b McCORMICK	10
3 Parks, H.	lbw b White	12	NOT OUT	29
4 Langridge, James	ST. BARNETT b BARNES	68		
5 H. T. Bartlett	c BARNES b WARD	157		
6 Cox, G.	b WARD	76		
7 A. J. Holmes (Capt.)	c BARNES b WHITE	13		
8 Hammond, H. E.	c McCORMICK b WHITE	8		
*9 Cornford, W	NOT OUT	12		
10 Wood, J.	ST. BARNETT b WARD	1		
11 Cornford, J.	ST. BARNETT b WARD	1		
	b 4 l b. 10 w n.b. 1	15	b l.b. w. 1 n.b.	1
	Total—	453	Total—	53

Runs at fall of wicket: 1-72 2-93 3-109 4-304 5-364 6-411 7-429 8-447 9-451 10-453
1-12 2-53 3- 4- 5- 6- 7- 8- 9- 10-

Bowling Analysis.	o.	m.	r.	w.	wd.	n.b.	o.	m.	r.	w.	wd.	n.b.
McCormick	24	1	86	0	...	...	6	0	18	1	...	...
Waite	17	4	55	0	...	...	4	2	5	0	...	...
McCabe	2	0	6	0	...	...	...	...	...	...	...	...
Ward	36.1	6	184	6	...	...	4.4	0	19	1	...	...
WHITE	33	13	75	3	...	...	...	...	...	...	...	...
BARNES	6	1	32	1	...	...	...	...	...	...	...	...

AUSTRALIANS	First Innings		Second Innings	
*1 C. W. Walker	b Hammond	7	NOT OUT	2
2 C. L. Badcock	c L'ridge, Js. b Wood	22	c HOLMES b WOOD	58
3 A. L. Hassett	b Hammond	74	c J. CORNFORD b WOOD	56
4 S. Barnes	lbw b Langridge, Js.	24	b WOOD	44
5 S. J. McCabe (Capt.)	b Wood	3	b HAMMOND	16
6 W. A. Brown	b Wood	75	c W. CORNFORD b HAMMOND	23
7 B. A. Barnett	c H'mond b L'ridge. Jn.	17	LBW b HAMMOND	53
8 M. G. Waite	c Stainton b C'nford, J.	46	b HAMMOND	9
9 E. S. White	c Stainton b Wood	44	b HAMMOND	15
10 F. Ward	c Hammond b C'ford, J.	2	c W. b J. CORNFORD	0
11 E. L. McCormick	not out	8	LBW b JAMES LANGRIDGE	2
	b 6 l b 5 w 3 n.b.	14	b. 13 l b. 8 w. 1 n.b.	22
	Total—	336	Total—	300

Runs at fall of wicket: 1-24 2-46 3-105 4-110 5-162 6-191 7-262 8-309 9-313 10-336
1-5 2-55 3-91 4-174 5-200 6-200 7-233 8-240 9-276 10-300

Bowling Analysis.	o.	m.	r.	w.	wd.	n.b.	o.	m.	r.	w.	wd.	n.b.
Cornford, J.	29	4	84	2	...	...	26	6	55	1	...	...
Hammond	32	6	86	2	3	...	34	4	107	5	...	...
Wood	25·4	1	96	4	...	...	25.4	3	81	3	...	...
Langridge, Js	18	4	49	1	...	..	1.2	7	35	1	...	...
Langridge, Jn.	2	..	7	1	...	...	...	...	...	...	...	...

*Wicket Keeper Umpires Russell & H. W. Lee. Scorers—E. Killick & W. Ferguson

Next Match on this Ground—Aug. 31, Sept. 1, 2, SUSSEX v. YORKSHIRE

Printed on the Ground by H. CROWHURST, Printer to the S.C.C.C., 50 Market Street, Brighton

SUSSEX v. DERBYSHIRE

28, 29 and 30 June 1939 | County Championship
Derby

When Sussex came to play Derbyshire at the end of June, they had not been faring particularly well. Just 3 wins from 15 first-class matches, including a defeat by Oxford University, was not an enviable record.

They appeared to be heading for another defeat at Derby when, on the last day, they snatched a quite sensational victory. The County's first innings had been no more than adequate, John Langridge and Hugh Bartlett making half-centuries, but a total of 258, even allowing for the vagaries of the Derby wicket, where the ball often kept low and occasionally lifted nastily, was not exceptional. The two Jacks, Duffield and Nye, did their best to put the County back on track. Nye took the host's three top-order wickets, breaking the bail and sending it about twenty yards when he bowled Stan Worthington, while the twenty-one-year-old medium-pacer Duffield, who had also contributed precious runs in the Sussex innings, took the last 5 wickets to fall. They went down for 21 runs and Duffield, in fact, took them in 11 deliveries without conceding a run. Despite the County enjoying a first-innings lead of 60, their second innings broke down badly in face of the pace of George and Alfred Pope and the leg-breaks and googlies of Tommy Mitchell, so that Derbyshire began the final day requiring an attainable 208 for victory.

Although the pitch certainly favoured the bowlers, so well did Worthington pull and cut that, when he was third out for 119 with the total on 185, Derbyshire needed a mere 23 runs for victory. They scored, in fact, only another 9 runs. James Langridge, in taking 5 wickets for 3 runs, did the hat-trick when he dismissed Rhodes, Hounsfield and Alfred Pope, and actually claimed his five victims – four in one over – without conceding a run in 11 deliveries. Curiously, this was precisely what Duffield had done on the previous day. At the other end, Nye sent back the last three batsmen in the course of 5 balls. The fourth, fifth, sixth and seventh Derby wickets went down with the score on 191 and, by another strange coincidence, it was on this very same score that the home side collapsed in their first innings. The County's bowlers were certainly the heroes of this remarkable win, although 'Tich' Cornford, with 5 catches behind the stumps, undoubtedly played his part in this scintillating victory against the odds.

Immediately after the end of this remarkable match, in which 18 'ducks' (two not out) were recorded from the 40 wickets that fell, a terrific hailstorm broke over the ground. Sussex had made it just in time!

James Langridge took a hat-trick.

Jack Nye bowled well.

Sussex won the toss and elected to bat

SUSSEX

	1st innings		2nd innings	
John Langridge	c Smith b Copson	85	c Worthington b Mitchell	39
J.H. Parks	b Copson	15	lbw b A.V. Pope	3
H.W. Parks	c Elliott b A.V. Pope	10	c Worthington b Copson	4
G. Cox	b Copson	0	c and b A.V. Pope	5
Jas. Langridge	lbw b Copson	0	lbw b G.H. Pope	27
*Mr H.T. Bartlett	c Elliott b Rhodes	93	c and b Mitchell	39
Mr R.A.A. Holt	b Rhodes	0	b G.H. Pope	9
C. Oakes	lbw b Rhodes	8	b G.H. Pope	0
#W. Cornford	c Worthington b Copson	5	lbw b Mitchell	0
J. Duffield	c Elliott b Copson	33	not out	20
J. K. Nye	not out	1	b Mitchell	0
Extras	(b5, lb3)	8	(lb1)	1
TOTAL		258		147

Bowling	O	M	R	W	O	M	R	W
Copson	20.4	4	64	6	7	2	16	1
A.V. Pope	18	2	71	1	6	1	19	2
G.H. Pope	12	0	55	0	12	1	49	3
Mitchell	4	0	22	0	9	1	45	4
Rhodes	10	0	38	3	4	0	17	0

DERBYSHIRE

	1st innings		2nd innings	
A.E. Alderman	c Cornford b Nye	15	c Cornford b Duffield	30
D. Smith	b Nye	81	c Cornford b Duffield	0
T.S. Worthington	b Nye	0	c Cornford b Jas Langridge	119
L.F. Townsend	c H. Parks b J. Parks	29	c Cornford b Nye	28
G.H. Pope	lbw b Duffield	37	c J.Parks b Jas Langridge	1
A.E. Rhodes	c Nye b Jas Langridge	8	c John Langridge b Jas Langridge	0
* Mr T.D. Hounsfield	b Duffield	12	c J.Parks b Jas Langridge	0
A.V. Pope	lbw b Duffield	0	c Cornford b Jas Langridge	0
#H. Elliott	lbw b Duffield	0	not out	0
T.B. Mitchell	not out	0	b Nye	0
W. Copson	b Duffield	0	b Nye	0
Extras	(b2 lb 14)	16	(b12, lb2, w1, nb 1)	16
TOTAL		198		194

Bowling	O	M	R	W	O	M	R	W
Nye	16	0	73	3	15	1	69	3
Duffield	10.5	1	38	5	14	0	78	2
J.H. Parks	16	7	33	1	5	0	28	0
Jas. Langridge	9	1	36	1	3	1	3	5
Cox	1	0	2	0				

Umpires: A. Dolphin and H. Ellliott

Sussex won by 13 runs

Sussex *v.* Yorkshire

30, 31 August and 1 September 1939 — County Championship
Hove

With the clouds of war hanging over the Brighton and Hove Cricket Week – otherwise a wholly enjoyable occasion – Yorkshire came to their match with Sussex at the end of August 1939 on the back of innings victories over Kent and Hampshire, and with another County Championship under their belt. It was their third successive Championship and the seventh time in the 1930s that they had come out on top.

This prestigious match had been chosen for Jim Parks' benefit, but an air of tension hung over the teams on the Wednesday morning, as 'Jack' Holmes won the toss for Sussex and elected to bat. The County had enjoyed only a moderately successful season and were to end up in tenth place, two places lower than in the previous season. The wicket, however, was perfect and Sussex posted 387, the highest total of the season against Yorkshire. This was due mainly to a quite scintillating innings from George Cox who, after a few risky shots, drove and cut for three hours and twenty minutes, scoring 28 fours, and 1 six off Hedley Verity, who had an uncharacteristically poor analysis, his eighteen 8-ball overs (a 1939 experiment) costing 6 runs each. Yorkshire lost Wilfred Barber early on, but at the close of play, with the visitors on 112 for 1 wicket, nearly 500 runs had been scored in a day of glorious cricket, although all round the ground people were listening to wireless sets in the hope that the last-minute efforts to secure peace might be successful.

Overnight, a thunderstorm flooded the ground, and play did not re-start until 3.30 p.m. on the Thursday. On the now rain-affected wicket, England's master batsman, Len Hutton, batted with remarkable skill and at no time allowed James Langridge's left-arm spin to take advantage of the conditions, as Yorkshire ended the day on 330 for 3. Shortly before 6.00 a.m. on the Friday, the news came through that Hitler had invaded Poland and that war was now a certainty. At Old Trafford, Lancashire's game with Surrey was called off, and the Yorkshire committee wired Brian Sellers and asked him to do the same, but since the match was for Jim Parks' benefit, play was continued. Hutton fell to Cox's medium-pace and, although Norman Yardley, who was ninth out, also reached a hundred, the last 7 Yorkshire wickets fell for 62 runs. When Sussex came to bat for a second time, the sun was blazing down and the wicket made for Verity's skills. In fewer than 12 overs, Sussex had capitulated to 33 all out and Verity, with 7 for 9, had achieved one of the best analyses of his career, bettered perhaps only by his two 10-wicket hauls. By mid-afternoon, the coach carrying the Yorkshire team homeward was on its way. Many of those who played in this match took a full part in the service of England in the Second World War: only Verity, the hero of the day, would not survive it.

Left: Jim Parks senior and his opening partners. *Right:* George Cox junior (left) and 'Jack' Holmes continue the Sussex innings.

YORKSHIRE WON BY 9 WICKETS

This Card does not necessarily include the fall of the last wicket.

2d. SUSSEX COUNTY CRICKET GROUND, HOVE, 2d.

Aug. 30, 31, Sept. 1, 1939. SUSSEX v. YORKSHIRE Sussex won toss

Hours of Play: **1st day, 11.30 to 7.0 2nd, 11.30 to 7.0 3rd, 11.0 to 4.30 or 5.0**

Lunch at 1.30. Tea at 4.30.

SUSSEX	First Innings		Second Innings	
1 R. G. Stainton	c. Wood b. Bowes	14	absent hurt	0
2 Langridge, John	run out	60	c Sellers b Robinson	3
3 Parks, H.	c. Wood b. Smailes	35	c Hutton b Verity	9
4 Cox, G	c. Smailes b. Robinson	198	c Wood b Verity	9
5 Langridge, James	c. Mitchell b. Bowes	17	c Mitchell b Verity	0
6 Parks, J.	c. Robinson b. Smailes	2	lbw b Verity	0
7 H. T. Bartlett	b. Robinson	24	b Verity	3
8 A. J. Holmes (Capt.)	b. Verity	11	b Verity	4
9 S. C. Griffith	c. Smailes b. Verity	17	b Verity	1
10 Nye, J.	not out	2	not out	3
11 Wood, J.	lbw b. Robinson	0	run out	0
	b. 3 l.b. 4 w. n.b. 7		b 1 l.b. w. n.b.	1
	Total—	387	Total—	33

Runs at fall of wicket { 1- 26 2- 89 3- 133 4- 202 5- 205 6- 266 7- 321 8- 361 9- 387 10- 387
{ 1- 0 2- 12 3- 12 4- 13 5- 19 6- 23 7- 8- 30 9- 33 10-

Bowling Analysis.	o.	m.	r.	w.	wd.	n.b.	o.	m.	r.	w.	wd.	n.b.
Bowes	17	0	71	2								
Smailes	12	0	48	2								
Yardley	9	0	48	0								
Verity	18	1	108	2			6	1	9	7		
Robinson	15	2	87	3			5.3	0	23	1		
Hutton	4	0	18	0								

YORKSHIRE.	First Innings		Second Innings	
1 Hutton, L.	lbw b Cox	103	c Griffith b Jas Langridge	1
2 Barber, W.	c. Griffith b. Nye	22	not out	18
3 Mitchell, A.	c Jas Langridge b Holmes	67	not out	11
4 Leyland, M.	c Sub b J Parks	64		
5 N. W. D Yardley	c H b Jas Langridge	108		
6 A. B Sellers (C)	c Bartlett b J Parks	12		
7 Smailes, F.	b J. Parks	0		
*8 Wood, A.	c Wood b Jas Langridge	2		
9 Robinson, E.	b Jas Langridge	0		
10 Verity, H.	not out	7		
11 Bowes, W.	c J Parks b Jas Langridge	2		
	b. 3 l.b. 1 w. 1 n.b 5		b. l b. w. n.b.	
	Total—	392	(1 wkt) Total—	30

Runs at fall of wicket { 1- 52 2- 175 3- 204 4- 342 5- 363 6- 364 7- 377 8- 377 9- 386 10- 392
{ 1- 4 2- 3- 4- 5- 6- 7- 8- 9- 10-

Bowling Analysis.	o.	m.	r.	w.	wd.	n.b.	o.	m.	r.	w.	wd.	n.b.
Nye	19	1	104	1								
Parks (J)	33	3	120	3			6.6	1	21	0		
Wood	10	1	30	0								
Jas Langridge	20.4	5	84	4			6	0	9	1		
Cox	10	2	34	1								
Holmes	3	0	15	1								

*Wicket Keeper Umpires—Hills & Parker Scorers—E. Killick & W. Ringrose

Next Match—Sept. 8, LADIES v. S. C. & GROUND, Admission Free.

Printed on the Ground by H. CROWHURST, Printer to the S.C.C.C. 50-2 Market Street, Brighton 1.

SUSSEX *v.* GLAMORGAN

19, 21 and 22 July 1947 — County Championship
Hove

Sussex had finished at the bottom of the County Championship in 1946, causing 'Billy' Griffith to realise that the post of captain/secretary was too much of a burden and to hand over the captaincy to his friend, Hugh Bartlett, for the 1947 season. By July, five wins had been secured and a sixth was added in the Glamorgan game at Hove.

The start of the match did not bode well for Sussex. The Glamorgan openers, Emrys Davies and Arnold Dyson, both reached hundreds and together put on 236 for the first wicket, but some good fast-bowling by 'Paddy' Carey, which included a hat-trick and was backed up well by Gordon Hurst's leg-breaks, finished the visitors' innings with the addition of a further 54 runs. It should have been a fillip to the Sussex side, but the batting, apart from a solid John Langridge innings, was woeful and the County were dismissed for exactly half their opponents' total, escaping the follow-on by the skin of their teeth.

Glamorgan batted soundly in their second knock and, declaring with 7 wickets down, set Sussex 376 to win. The visitors' skipper, Wilf Wooller, a man not noted for a soft approach to the game, must have felt relatively assured of an easy victory. He had, however, not reckoned on the brilliance of George Cox. In the first innings, Cox had been pressed into opening, an area of cricket which was not suited to his flamboyant style, and had been dismissed cheaply. He was, therefore, put down the order in the second innings, and when he arrived at the wicket 3 wickets were already down for 40 runs. John Langridge, Charlie Oakes and Robert Hunt were already back in the pavilion. Cox began to attack the Glamorgan attack at once and, driving and cutting beautifully, he gradually started to master the bowling. At the other end, Harry Parks, who had come in at number three, was batting soundly and the pair added 219 for the fourth wicket, completely altering the balance of the game, before Parks was dismissed just 4 runs short of his century. There was, however, still much to do. Another 117 runs were still needed, but Cox, now in partnership with his captain, went on relentlessly, so that by the time his double hundred came up, the County, after their poor start, were home and dry for the loss of only one more wicket. Cox had played a magnificent innings lasting four-and-a-quarter hours, in which he had hit 1 five and 21 fours.

Although they lost the return game with Glamorgan at Cardiff by 4 wickets, Sussex went on to record a further 3 victories in 1947, finishing in equal ninth place with Glamorgan in the Championship – a vast improvement on their dismal performance in the previous year.

George Cox junior, scorer of a double hundred.

Sussex *v.* Glamorgan

This Card does not necessarily include the fall of the last wicket.

3d. SUSSEX COUNTY CRICKET GROUND HOVE. **3d.**

July 19, 21 22, 1947. SUSSEX v. GLAMORGAN. Glamorgan won toss

Hours of Play: 1st day, 12.0. to 7.0 2nd, 12.0 to 7.0 3rd, 11.30 to 6.0 or 6.30
Lunch at 1.30. to 2.10 Tea Interval 4.30. to 4.45

SUSSEX.	First Innings		Second Innings	
1 Langridge, John	b Wooller	47	b Wooller	3
2 Cox, G.	b Wooller	2	not out	205
3 Parks, H. W.	c H. Davies b Lavis	9	c Davies, E. b Muncer	96
4 Oakes C	st Davies, H. b Edwards	15	c Porter b Lavis	16
5 R. G. Hunt	c Davies. H. b Davies, E.	1	b Edwards	2
6 H. T. Bartlett (Capt)	c Watkins b Edwards	5	c Lavis b Muncer	38
7 Smith, D V.	st Davies, H. b Wooller	29	not out	7
*8 S. C. Griffith	lbw b Wooller	9		
9 Carey, P. A.	c Dyson b Lavis	2		
10 Hurst, G. T.	c Muncer b Wooller	3		
11 Cornford, J.	not out	10		
	b.9 l.b.4 w. n.b.	13	b.8 l.b.1 w. n.b.	9
	Total	145	(5 WKTS) Total	376

Runs at fall of wicket									
1-9	2-30	3-52	4-79	5-86	6-88	7-101	8-112	9-132	10-145
1-5	2-5	3-40	4-259	5-354	6-	7-	8-	9-	10-

Bowling Analysis	o.	m.	r.	w.	wd.	n.b.	o.	m.	r.	w.	wd.	n.b.
Wooller	25.3	8	58	5	..	..	27	5	98	1	..	..
Edwards	11	3	34	2	..	..	10	1	37	1	..	..
Lavis	9	3	14	2	..	..	10	4	35	1	..	..
Muncer	8	4	12	..	..	..	21.5	3	89	2	..	..
Davies, E.	16	9	14	1	..	..	28	8	72	..	..	..
Porter	..	..	..	..	..	..	4	1	16	..	..	..
Jones	..	..	..	..	..	..	7	2	20	..	..	..

GLAMORGAN.	First Innings.		Second Innings.	
1 Dyson, A.	c Jn. L'gridge b Carey	118	lbw b Cornford	10
2 Davies, E.	c Griffith b Carey	105	b Carey	50
3 Jones, W. E.	b Hurst	25	c Jn. L'gridge b Carey	4
4 A. Porter	lbw b Hurst	0	c Griffith b Carey	0
5 Watkins, A.	b Hurst,	4	lbw b Hurst	19
6 M. Robinson	b Hurst	4	run out	16
7 W. Wooller(Capt.)	c and b Carey	11	c Griffith b Cornford	34
8 Muncer, L.	lbw b Hurst	0	not out	53
9 Lavis, G.	not out	2	not out	19
10*Davies, H.	b Carey	0	Innings declared	
11 A. M. Edwards	c Griffith b Carey	0		
	b.14 l.b.5 w.1 n.b.	20	b.4 l.b.1 w. n.b	5
	Total	290	(7 WKTS DEC) Total	230

Runs at fall of wicket									
1-236	2-241	3-248	4-258	5-273	6-282	7-282	8-290	9-290	10-290
1-18	2-39	3-39	4-83	5-119	6-125	7-186	8-	9-	10-

Bowling Analysis	o.	m.	r.	w.	wd.	n.b.	o.	m.	r.	w.	wd.	n.b.
Cornford	21	7	45	..	..	..	22	5	53	2	..	..
Carey	18.2	3	45	5	..	..	22	2	98	3	..	..
Cox	21	4	37	..	..	..	8	4	10	..	..	..
Hurst	30	7	68	5	..	..	15	4	41	1	..	..
C. Oakes	17	3	56	..	..	..	5	..	23	..	..	..
Smith	3	..	10	..	..	..	..	..	..	..	..	..
Bartlett	1	..	4	..	1	..	..	..	..	..	..	..
Hunt	1	..	5	..	..	..	..	..	..	..	..	..

*Wicket Keeper. Umpires- Harris & Coleman Scorers-W. Locke & A. Allen

Next Match at Hove, Aug. 2, 4, 5, SUSSEX v. MIDDLESEX. Js. L'ridge Benefit

SUSSEX WON BY 5 WICKETS

SUSSEX *v.* KENT

23, 25 and 26 June 1951 — County Championship
Tunbridge Wells

Jim Parks junior had announced himself to Sussex fans and the cricketing public in general in 1950 when, at the age of eighteen and batting at number seven in the order, he had scored a magnificent 159* against Kent at Gillingham. Now, a year later, on the green and leafy Nevill Ground in Tunbridge Wells with superb rhododendrons in bloom, he again set about the Kent bowling.

Sussex made a slow start and, when Don Smith had been caught at first slip off acting Kent captain, Simon Kimmins, Parks joined John Langridge and slowly they began to master the Kent bowlers. The first hour produced a miserly 25 runs during which time Kimmins had conceded a mere 3 runs in 9 overs. When former England leg-spinner, Douglas Wright, came on to bowl, Parks hit him for a consecutive four and six, but this occasioned a bowling change and Brian Edrich removed John Langridge just after the fifty had been reached. This brought Sussex skipper, James Langridge, to join Parks and that concluded Kent's success for the day. The pair batted consistently throughout the Saturday afternoon and evening, and Parks reached his hundred after batting for three hours and twenty-five minutes, while Langridge took five minutes longer. By the close, Sussex were well set on 325 for 2 wickets.

After the Sunday rest-day – a feature not seen nowadays – the pair continued where they had left off. After twenty minutes, Parks passed his 159 of the previous season and the pair had added 294 in four and three-quarter hours when Langridge, who had struck 15 fours, was caught at the wicket off Wright. Their third-wicket stand failed by only 4 runs to equal the previous Sussex third-wicket partnership, made between Ranjitsinhji and Ernest Killick against Lancashire at Hove in 1901. Parks moved on towards his double hundred, but 12 runs short he too was taken at the wicket from the bowling of the off-spinner, Ray Dovey. Altogether he had batted for six and a quarter hours and had hit 2 sixes and 13 fours.

Kent faced a formidable task and, although Arthur Fagg and Peter Hearn enjoyed a sound second-wicket partnership, Ted James and Alan Oakman caused a middle-order collapse when 4 wickets went down for the addition of a single. Reaching a meagre 156, Kent were forced to follow-on, but against the pace of Jim Wood and Jim Cornford, they fared even less well than in the first innings. By the close, they had lost 8 wickets and still needed 104 runs to make the visitors bat again. Edrich held on well and reached his half-century, but Sussex were home and dry before lunch on the final day.

The Nevill Ground in Tunbridge Wells during the Kent first innings.

SUSSEX WON BY AN INNINGS AND 94 RUNS

This card does not necessarily include the fall of the last wicket.

Tunbridge Wells Cricket Week, 1951

KENT v. SUSSEX, June 23rd, 25th & 26th, 1951

Sussex won the toss. PRICE: THREEPENCE

SUSSEX:—	1st Innings		2nd Innings	
1 Langridge (John)	c Fagg b Edrich	25		
2 Smith D V	c Page b Kimmins	7		
3 Parks J	c Fenner b Dovey	188		
*4 Langridge (James)	c Fenner b Wright	144		
5 Cox G	not out	13		
6 Oakes J	c Fagg b Edrich	1		
7 Oakman A				
8 James A E				
†9 Webb R				
10 Wood J				
11 Cornford J				
	b 5; lb 6; nb...; w...	11	b...; lb...; nb...; w...	
Umpires: F. Chester & A. Skelding	(5 wkts dec) Total	389	Total	

1 wkt. for 16 2- 58 3- 352 4- ... 5- ... 6- ... 7- ... 8- ... 9- ... 10- ...

1 wkt. for ... 2- ... 3- ... 4- ... 5- ... 6- ... 7- ... 8- ... 9- ... 10- ...

Bowling Analysis:	O	M	R	W	Nb	Wd	O	M	R	W	Nb	Wd
Page	21	4	52	0								
Kimmins	26	8	51	1								
Wright	28	4	92	1								
Dovey	36	7	97	1								
Edrich	19.4	3	47	2								
Hearn	3	0	24	0								
Cowdrey	3	0	15	0								

KENT:—	1st Innings		2nd Innings	
1 Fagg A E	c Oakman b James	49	b Wood	2
2 Phebey A H	c Webb b Cornford	9	lbw b Cornford	0
3 Hearn P	c Parks b Oakman	32	c & b Oakes	40
4 M. C. Cowdrey	b James	0	b Wood	4
5 Mayes R	b Oakman	1	c Webb b Wood	2
6 Edrich B R	c John Langridge b Oakman	1	not out	56
*7 S E A Kimmins	b Oakman	25	lbw b Cornford	0
†8 M D Fenner	c Jas Langridge b Oakman	5	c John Langridge b Cornford	0
9 Dovey R R	c Parks b Jas Langridge	10	st Webb b Oakes	6
10 Wright D V P	not out	12	b Cornford	11
11 Page J C T	b James	7	b Cornford	6
	b 4; lb...; nb 1; w...	5	b 8; lb 3; nb 1; w...	12
Scorers: W. R. Locke & E. Hoskin	Total	156	Total	139

* Capt. † Wicketkeeper

1 wkt. for 12 2- 91 3- 91 4- 92 5- 92 6- 99 7- ... 8- ... 9- ... 10- ...

1 wkt. for ... 2- ... 3- ... 4- ... 5- ... 6- ... 7- ... 8- ... 9- ... 10- ...

Bowling Analysis:	O	M	R	W	Nb	Wd	O	M	R	W	Nb	Wd
Wood	8	0	29	0			9	0	43	3		
Cornford	10	1	29	1			13.2	4	36	5		
Oakman	21	8	34	5			7	3	7	0		
James	14.1	6	32	3			11	3	23	0		
James Langridge	4	1	17	1								
Oakes							12	6	18	2		

FLATS: White at 55 overs. Yellow at 60 overs. White & Yellow at 65 overs, New Ball due.

HOURS OF PLAY: First two days, 11-30 to 6.30 p.m. Third day, 11.0 to 6 or 6.30 p.m. with extra half-hour on third day if demanded. LUNCH, 1.30 to 2.10 p.m.

Printed by Messrs. Clements & Son (Tun. Wells), Ltd., Grove Hill Road, Tunbridge Wells.

Sussex v. Leicestershire

6, 7 and 8 June 1953 — County Championship
Leicester

David Sheppard's one year as Sussex skipper was a season of great success. For the sixth time in the twentieth century – one more occasion was to follow in 1981 – they reached second place in the Championship. The reason is not hard to find: although James Langridge, appointed the County's first professional captain in 1950 after the uproarious AGM of that spring, had given stalwart service for three seasons, the appointment of Sheppard in his stead for 1953 was to prove a catalyst. Although he was only twenty-four and, therefore, much younger than many of the men he was to lead, he was held in the high esteem which allows a man to take the reins whatever the relevant ages. It was only sad, at least for the County's fortunes, that Sheppard had given himself the one full season before entering the Church of England.

Although Sheppard would have been the first to declare that Sussex's success in 1953 was all teamwork, many would see his own outstanding batsmanship at the top of the order, usually in conjunction with the forty-three-year-old John Langridge, and his fearless fielding close to the wicket as principal reasons for the County's success. When Sussex came to Leicester in early June for their seventh Championship match, they had won only one of their previous engagements, and the fact that they added a second was due firstly to the desire of the home captain, Charles Palmer, to force a result and, secondly, to Sheppard's magnificent second innings. On the opening day, when the pitch showed some early life, the Leicester batsmen were initially somewhat restrained, but Maurice Tompkin mastered the conditions and his 150 was the keystone of the home side's substantial first innings. When Sussex came to bat, Sheppard and John Langridge showed enterprise in adding 97 for the first wicket, but the later batting, apart from Jim Parks' well-made 53, was more panache than substance and the County had a deficit of 109 on the first innings.

As the second innings began, Leicestershire were firmly in the driving seat and, after Tompkin and Palmer had added 128 for the third wicket, the latter was able to declare with 6 wickets down and leave himself four hours in which to bowl Sussex out for a second time. Seen from a different perspective, it gave the visitors a chance to reach 346 in a little more than 70 overs at a rate of nearly 5 runs per over. Sussex were ready for it, and Sheppard and John Langridge opened with a partnership of 153. After the latter's dismissal, partnerships of 85 and 108 with George Cox and Charlie Oakes respectively allowed the Sussex captain to bring his side home with a chance-less innings. Finally, he was just 14 runs short of his double hundred and had struck a six, a five and 20 fours. It was very much the stuff of Sheppard's year in charge.

David Sheppard (left) with George Cox junior.

Leicestershire won the toss and elected to bat

LEICESTERSHIRE

G. Lester	c Sheppard b Oakman	20	lbw b Thomson	12
G.A. Smithson	lbw b James	28	b Thomson	18
M. Tompkin	c Sheppard b Cox	150	c Suttle b Oakman	69
*C.H. Palmer	lbw b Oakman	22	st Webb b James	79
V.E. Jackson	c Langridge b Wood	46	c James b Oakman	16
V.S. Munden	b Wood	24	not out	26
M.R. Hallam	lbw b Oakes	47	b James	9
J.E. Walsh	run out	15	not out	7
#J. Firth	not out	3		
C.T. Spencer	not out	3		
J. Goodwin	did not bat			
Extras	(b5, lb8)	13		
TOTAL	(for 8 wkts dec.)	371	(for 6 wkts dec)	236

1/51,2/51,3/90,4/219,5/263,6/314,7/357,8/368   1/29,2/30,3/158,4/190,5/195,6/227

Bowling	O	M	R	W	O	M	R	W
Wood	24	8	53	2	11	1	34	0
Thomson	21	6	59	0	16	4	51	2
Oakman	41	9	106	2	18	0	80	2
James	28	8	63	1	17	4	60	2
Parks	1	0	8	0				
Oakes	8	2	21	1				
Cox	18	4	48	1	4	1	11	0

SUSSEX

*D.S. Sheppard	c and b Walsh	48	not out	186
John Langridge	c Lester b Walsh	46	st Firth b Munden	65
G. Cox	c Lester b Walsh	0	c and b Munden	36
C. Oakes	lbw b Walsh	8	n ot out	48
J.M. Parks	b Goodwin	53		
K.G. Suttle	c Tompkin b Spencer	24		
A.S.M. Oakman	b Spencer	2		
N.I. Thomson	c Hallam b Spencer	22		
A.E. James	lbw b Spencer	1		
D.J. Wood	b Walsh	16		
#R.T. Webb	not out	18		
Extras	(b9, lb6, nb9)	24	(lb8, nb3)	11
TOTAL		262	(for 2 wkts)	346

1/97,2/97,3/107,4/114,5/165,6/171,7/203,8/212,9/229   1/153,2/238

Bowling	O	M	R	W	O	M	R	W
Spencer	22	4	58	4	13	1	70	0
Goodwin	13	2	35	1	12	1	51	0
Jackson	24	11	57	0	4	0	28	0
Walsh	34.4	5	88	5	10	1	40	0
Munden	2	2	0	0	21	0	88	2
Palmer					15	0	58	0

Umpires: T.J. Bartley and E. Cooke

Sussex won by 8 wickets

SUSSEX *v.* GLOUCESTERSHIRE

8, 9 and 10 May 1957 County Championship
Hove

Don Smith hit magnificently.

Jessop in 1903, Alletson in 1911 and Hugh Bartlett in 1938 – over the seasons there have been some splendid whirlwind innings played at Hove, and fifty-four years after the first one came another, Don Smith's 166 against Gloucestershire in the County's first encounter of that season.

The visitors took the first innings and posted a sound 322, with Derek Hawkins scoring a maiden hundred and earning himself a County cap. When it came to Sussex's turn, they found run-making difficult against the accurate slow-bowling of Sam Cook and 'Bomber' Wells – not to be confused, of course, with Sussex's own version of that ilk in the 1980s and 1990s! Leslie Lenham, aged twenty and playing only his second game for the County, was unfortunate not to emulate Hawkins, but on 95 he played the ball onto his foot from where it went straight into the hands of short-leg. With a first-innings lead of 43, the West Country side batted confidently in their second innings and, when they declared just after lunch on the third day, they left Sussex to score 267 in three and a quarter hours.

At the end of eighty minutes, Don Smith and Lenham had made only 81 together and the task looked now well out of the County's reach. Then Smith transformed the game with what Sussex cricket historian, John Marshall, has rightly described as 'an innings of electrifying brilliance'. From 58 balls bowled after tea, Sussex scored 82 runs – 74 from Smith's bat – in twenty-seven minutes. He hit 8 sixes and 4 fours from the 34 balls he received, and moved from 48 to 104 in nineteen minutes while 28 balls were bowled. The first wicket did not fall until 163 had been reached and, although Ken Suttle was run out, Smith continued to flay the bowling. Before he fell lbw, he had hit 9 sixes and 11 fours out of 253 in 175 minutes. With eight minutes to spare, Sussex romped home by 7 wickets.

Comparisons are never a good thing. It is true that Alletson made 189 in ninety minutes, Bartlett nearly struck the tavern with a six and Jessop hit a ball over the old South Stand, but Smith's innings was one of great ferocity and must rank among the hardest-hit innings that Hove has ever witnessed. The boundary was fairly short on the pavilion side and most of his sixes landed there, one striking a member who, sadly, had to be taken to hospital.

This was Don Smith's year. Aged thirty-four and the senior professional in his thirteenth season, he now found his ability recognised by England. In June, he made 147* against the touring West Indians and found himself opening the England innings in three of that summer's Test matches.

Gloucestershire won the toss and elected to bat

GLOUCESTERSHIRE

D.M. Young	c Webb b Bates	12	b Marlar	30
D. Carpenter	st Webb b Marlar	36	c sub Smith	48
T.W. Graveney	c Potter b Marlar	37	c Bates b Smith	35
R.B. Nicholls	lbw b Smith	26	st Webb b James	54
*G.M. Emmett	c Smith b Suttle	39	c Potter b Marlar	12
D.G. Hawkins	c Smith b Suttle	106	b James	13
G.E. Lambert	b Suttle	8	c Lenham b James	4
D.R. Smith	c Lenham b Thomson	4	not out	4
#P. Rochford	lbw b Thomson	0		
C. Cook	not out	35		
B.D. Wells	c Webb b Thomson	4		
Extras	(b10, lb1, nb4)	15	(b19, lb3, nb1)	23
TOTAL		322	(for 7 wkts dec.)	223

1/27 2/77 3/97 4/135 5/173 6/193 7/215 8/215 9/305 (3.06 an over)

1/72 2/131 3/132 4/148 5/205 6/215 7/223

Bowling	O	M	R	W	O	M	R	W
Bates	25	5	74	1	10	2	30	0
Thomson	20.1	6	70	3	6	3	11	0
James	8	2	27	0	5.2	1	21	3
Marlar	10	3	32	2	31	13	72	2
Suttle	20	6	43	3	14	2	40	0
Smith	19	5	52	1	15	4	26	2
Parks	3	1	9	0				

SUSSEX

D.V. Smith	c and b Wells	40	lbw b Lambert	166
L.J. Lenham	c Lambert b Wells	95	st Rochford b Cook	34
K.G. Suttle	b Cook	48	run out	12
J.M. Parks	c Hawkins b Cook	40	not out	27
G. Potter	b Wells	0		
N.I. Thomson	c Carpenter b Cook	16		
D.J. Foreman	c Graveney b Cook	0	not out	10
#R.T. Webb	not out	20		
A.E. James	c Smith b Wells	1		
D.L. Bates	c Rochford b Cook	7		
*R.G. Marlar	c Lambert b Cook	2		
Extras	(b5, lb4, nb1)	10	(b6, lb13)	19
TOTAL		279	(for 3 wkts)	268

1/72 2/161 3/209 4/209 5/237 6/237 7/254 8/262 9/277 (2.7 an over)

1/163 2/185 3/253

Bowling	O	M	R	W	O	M	R	W
Lambert	9	0	37	0	17	1	65	1
Smith	7	0	18	0	13.4	1	39	0
Wells	38	10	101	4	11	2	51	0
Cook	41.5	18	84	6	19	1	61	1
Hawkins	7	0	29	0	2	0	33	0

Umpires: F.S. Lee and L.H. Gray

Sussex won by 7 wickets

Sussex *v.* Middlesex

30 July, 1 and 2 August 1960 County Championship
Hove

Ted Dexter was one of the most exciting and high-achieving cricketers of his time – at Cambridge University, in his early and then his captaincy days with Sussex and, of course, with England, for whom he played on 62 occasions, 30 as captain. The Bank Holiday fixture with Middlesex in 1960, then a traditional part of the County calendar, was an occasion when his great versatility shone through. Sussex prospered in this first year of Dexter's captaincy, accomplishing the remarkably steep ascent from fifteenth to fourth place in the County Championship. Sussex won the toss and batted first in front of a large crowd, the County's innings being virtually all Dexter, as he struck 19 fours in an innings lasting five hours. Only a well-made 80 by Don Smith, who added 181 for the fifth wicket with his skipper, otherwise contributed greatly to the Sussex total. Middlesex, when their turn to bat came, had to deal with Ian Thomson at his best as he removed three of the top five and added another as the tail was finished off – the visitors' total hardly exceeding Dexter's own personal score.

With a healthy lead of 147, Sussex batted for a second time and, apart from another half-century from Smith, did little to distinguish themslves, but with their first-innings lead they were able to declare and leave Middlesex to make 329 to win in five hours – a tall order and potentially the highest innings score of the match. When the visitors were on 121 for 6 wickets, a storm erupted over Hove, and it looked as if it might save them from certain defeat, but it was possible for play to begin again with an hour's play still remaining. Dexter, who before the stoppage had taken 3 wickets for a single in the course of his second spell, then dismissed Fred Titmus and Don Bennett without addition to Middlesex's score. Ron Hooker, batting down the order, together with John Warr and Alan Moss and with no hope of winning the match, then played dead bats to a total of 82 deliveries from the bowling of Dexter, Thomson and Don Bates before Hooker pushed a single off Thomson. When Ron Bell picked up a brilliant catch at backward short-leg to dismiss the Middlesex captain, it meant that, in an 8-over spell, Dexter had taken 6 wickets for 1 run. Only thirteen minutes of the final hour remained as Sussex completed a comprehensive victory in what had proved to be a remarkable conclusion.

Sussex in 1960, from left to right, back row: K.G. Suttle, L.J. Lenham, N.I. Thomson, D.L. Bates, A. Buss, R.V. Bell, G.C. Cooper. Front row: D.J. Mordaunt, Rev. D.S. Sheppard, E.R. Dexter (captain), D.V. Smith, J.M. Parks.

SUSSEX WON BY 202 RUNS

This Card does not necessarily include the fall of the last wicket.

3d. ***Sussex County Cricket Ground, Hove*** **3d.**

SUSSEX v. MIDDLESEX

Saturday, Monday, & Tuesday, July 30th, August 1st & 2nd, 1960.

Hours of Play : 1st day ; 11.30-6.30 ; 2nd day ; 11.30-6.30 ; 3rd day 11 to 5.30 or 6

Lunch Interval : 1.30 to 2.10. Sussex won toss are batting

SUSSEX	1st Innings		2nd Innings	
1 A. S. M. Oakman	c Murray b Bennett	13	c WHITE b HOOKER	13
2 L. J. Lenham	b Warr	4	c MURRAY b HOOKER	5
3 †E. R. Dexter	b DRYBOROUGH	157	b TITMUS	26
4 *J. M. Parks	b Bennett	0	c MURRAY b BENNETT	21
5 K. G. Suttle	c Parfitt b Hooker	9	c WHITE b HOOKER	21
6 D. V. Smith	c PARFITT b BENNETT	80	NOT OUT	65
7 G. H. G. Doggart	NOT OUT	39	NOT OUT	20
8 Nawab of Pataudi	NOT OUT	18		
9 N. I. Thomson				
10 R. V. Bell				
11 D. L. Bates				
	b 2, lb 5, wb 1, nb , x	8	b , lb 9, wb 1, nb , x	10
Scoring Rate 3·00	(6 WKTS DEC) Total	328	(5 WKTS DEC) Total	181

Runs at fall 1- 6, 2- 26, 3- 27, 4- 42, 5-223, 6-294, 7- , 8- , 9- , 10-

of wicket : 1-18, 2-19, 3-67, 4-67, 5-136, 6- , 7- , 8- , 9- , 10-

Bowling Analysis	o	m	r	w	wb	nb	o	m	r	w	wb	nb
Moss	10	1	31	1								
Warr	20	5	49	1								
Bennett	21	2	58	3			20	2	65	1		
Hooker	19	4	58	1			20	7	70	3		
TITMUS	20	3	48	0			10	4	23	1		
DRYBROUGH	16	1	65	1			4	2	2	0		
GALE	3	0	11	0			1	0	11	0		

MIDDLESEX	1st Innings		2nd Innings	
1 W. E. Russell	c DEXTER b BATES	5	c BELL b DEXTER	11
2 R. A. Gale	RUN OUT	14	b BATES	33
3 R. A. White	c DEXTER b THOMSON	3	LBW b DEXTER	27
4 R. W. Hooker	c DOGGART b THOMSON	15	NOT OUT	5
5 P. H. Parfitt	c PARKS b THOMSON	49	b BATES	13
6 F. J. Titmus	RUN OUT	56	c BATES b DEXTER	27
7 D. Bennett	c SUTTLE b SMITH	4	b DEXTER	0
8 *J. T. Murray	b BATES	16	c PARKS b DEXTER	1
9 C. S. Drybrough	c BELL b SMITH	0	c PARKS b DEXTER	0
10 A. E. Moss	NOT OUT	6	c PARKS b THOMSON	0
11 †J. J. Warr	c BATES b THOMSON	12	c BELL b DEXTER	0
	b , lb , wb , nb 1, x	1	b 5, lb 3, wb , nb 1, x	9
Scoring Rate 2·40	Total	181	Total	126

Runs at fall 1-17, 2-23, 3-26, 4-45, 5-136, 6-147, 7-150, 8-150, 9-175, 10-181

of wicket : 1-27, 2-52, 3-68, 4-119, 5-120, 6-120, 7-121, 8-121, 9-121, 10-126

Bowling Analysis	o	m	r	w	wb	nb	o	m	r	w	wb	nb
THOMSON	26·1	11	50	4			22·1	13	26	1		
BATES	24	6	57	2			13	4	50	2		
DEXTER	7	0	24	0			18	11	24	7		
SUTTLE	1	1	0	0			3	2	6	0		
SMITH	9	1	27	2			5	1	11	0		
BELL	8	2	22	0								

†Captain *Wicket-keeper

Umpires : W. E. Phillipson & H. Elliott. Scorers : G. Washer & A. Alldis.

Please do not move about during delivery of an over.

SUSSEX *v.* WORCESTERSHIRE

7 September 1963 Gillette Final
Lord's

The sedate atmosphere of Lord's took on something of a carnival air when Sussex and Worcestershire contested the Gillette Cup in the first-ever limited-overs final. Coaches from the two counties had brought many of the 25,000 spectators to witness this wholly new contest, rosettes were on sale at the gates and, despite the dull weather, there was a feeling abroad that something important was about to happen. Worcestershire had overcome Surrey and Glamorgan in the early rounds, and Jack Flavell, with 6 for 14, had demolished Lancashire in the semi-final. Ken Suttle's 104 had taken Sussex past the three hundred-mark in their first-round match against Kent at Tunbridge Wells and, despite a hundred by Peter Richardson, the County had come out on top. They had won a close-fought encounter in the second round against Yorkshire at Hove when Jim Parks had contributed a brilliant 90. In the semi-final at Northampton, the County had been indebted to Ted Dexter's 115, made in a partnership of 160 in ninety-five minutes with Jim Parks, and to some clever bowling by Ian Thomson, all of which ensured success over the Midland county. Two relatively evenly-matched sides were, therefore, ready to contest the prize.

Ted Dexter, on winning the toss, decided to bat on a soft wicket and the County's normally free-scoring batsmen found the going difficult. The departure of Dexter for a meagre 3 caused a roar from the Worcestershire supporters that might well have come from a goal in the Cup Final at Wembley! The slow left-arm spin twins of Norman Gifford and Doug Slade, ably supported by Martin Horton's off-breaks, were in their element and, had it not been for Jim Parks' 57 (made in ninety minutes with 1 six and 4 fours), Sussex might well have failed to reach an acceptable total. The dull weather persisted throughout the day and by mid-afternoon, when Worcestershire, requiring only 2.5 runs per over to win,

Richard Langridge pulls a ball from Norman Gifford.

Sussex won by 14 runs

 **LORD'S**  **GROUND** 

Gillette Cup

FINAL OF THE KNOCK-OUT COMPETITION

SUSSEX v. WORCESTERSHIRE

Saturday, 7th September, 1963

SUSSEX

1	A. S. M. Oakman	c Slade b Gifford	19
2	R. J. Langridge	b Gifford	34
3	K. G. Suttle	b Gifford	9
†4	E. R. Dexter	c Broadbent b Horton	3
5	L. J. Lenham	c Booth b Gifford	7
*6	J. M. Parks	b Slade	57
7	G. C. Cooper	l b w b Slade	0
8	N. I. Thomson	l b w b Flavell	1
9	A. Buss	c Booth b Carter	3
10	J. A. Snow	b Flavell	10
11	D. L. Bates	not out	3
		B 9, l b 10, w , n-b 3,	22
		Total	168

FALL OF THE WICKETS

1—62 2—67 3—76 4—98 5—118 6—123 7—134 8—142 9—157 10—168

ANALYSIS OF BOWLING

Name	O.	M.	R.	W.	Wd.	N-b
Flavell	14.2	3	31	2	...	2
Carter	12	1	39	1	...	1
Slade	11	2	23	2	...	...
Gifford	15	4	33	4	...	...
Horton	8	1	20	1	...	...
...	...	...	...	...	...	...
...	...	...	...	...	...	...

WORCESTERSHIRE

†1	D. Kenyon	l b w b Buss	1
2	M. J. Horton	c and b Buss	26
3	R. G. A. Headley	c Snow b Bates	25
4	T. W. Graveney	c Dexter b Oakman	29
5	D. W. Richardson	c Parks b Thomson	3
6	R. G. Broadbent	c Bates b Snow	13
*7	R. Booth	not out	34
8	D. N. F. Slade	b Buss	3
9	N. Gifford	b Snow	0
10	J. A. Flavell	b Snow	0
11	R. G. M. Carter	run out	2
		B 8, l-b 9, w , n-b 2,	19
		Total	154

FALL OF THE WICKETS

1—7 2—36 3—80 4—91 5—103 6—128 7—132 8—133 9—133 10—154

ANALYSIS OF BOWLING

Name	O.	M.	R.	W.	Wd.	N-b
Thomson	13.2	4	35	1	...	...
Buss	15	2	39	3	...	...
Oakman	13	4	17	1	...	...
Suttle	5	2	11	0	...	...
Bates	9	2	20	1	...	2
Snow	8	0	13	3	...	...
...	...	...	...	...	...	...

Umpires—F. C. Gardner & F. S. Lee Scorers—G. W. Washer & W. Faithfull

† Captain * Wicket-keeper

Play begins at 11. Luncheon Interval 1 p.m.—1.30 p.m.

Tea Interval 4.30 p.m.—4.45 p.m. (may be varied according to state of game)

Sussex won the toss

Ted Dexter and Jim Parks – architects of Sussex's success in the early days of one-day cricket.

The crowd surge on to the field to witness the presentation.

set off on their chase, it was still anybody's game. Tony Buss, however, promptly disposed of the Worcester captain, Don Kenyon, and although Horton, Ron Headley and Tom Graveney all batted soundly, wickets fell steadily. Alan Oakman bowled a spell of his off-spin to line and length and, when the twenty-one-year-old John Snow came on and took three quick wickets, things were definitely going Sussex's way.

Wicketkeeper Roy Booth, however, was not going to go down without a fight and, in partnership with the last man, Bob Carter, added 21 precious runs in the gathering gloom before a run-out brought the Worcester innings to a close. The Sussex supporters, who had been cheering their side on to the strains of 'Sussex by the Sea' were ecstatic and swarmed onto the pitch to congregate in front of the pavilion. Here they saw Ted Dexter, having received the cup from MCC president Lord Nugent, hold it aloft to tumultuous cheers. Norman Gifford, the only bowler to take 4 wickets, was awarded the Man of the Match accolade – a significant choice in so far as medium pace short-of-a-length bowling had, up to this point, been regarded as an essential component of limited-overs cricket and was to presage the essential role that slow bowlers would take in later years.

Sussex's success was, of course, a team effort. The shrewd captaincy of Ted Dexter who had recognised, ahead of other contemporary County captains, that sixty to sixty-five overs represented a significant amount of cricket, that batting needed not be frenetic and that cleverly-set defensive fields had a part to play in one-day cricket, was to set Sussex on a successful path in Gillette and NatWest cricket – an area in which they have won more trophies than in any other form of the game.

Sussex *v.* Warwickshire

6, 8 and 9 June 1964 — County Championship
Worthing

The Manor Ground at Worthing, where the wicket was always regarded by players with some suspicion, is now no longer used by Sussex. In this match, in June 1964, where rain had additionally affected the surface, few batsmen came to terms with it and Ian Thomson, then aged thirty-five, enhanced even the earlier achievements of his illustrious career.

On Saturday, the first day of the match, Bob Barber and Mike Smith batted well in adding 55 for the third Warwickshire wicket, but the elements cut short the day's play with the visitors on 93 for 2 wickets. On the Monday, the weather was kinder, but not the wicket. By lunch, Thomson, who had begun his stint with 6 consecutive maidens, had 8 wickets for 30 and soon after had bagged all 10. Sussex did not make much of a fist of their innings and, although Ken Suttle batted solidly and John Snow and Ron Bell added 39 for the ninth wicket, the Warwickshire seam attack secured a 76-run advantage for their side. By the close, when the Midlanders had reached 44 for 4 in their second innings, 267 runs had been scored in the day for the loss of 22 wickets.

The Tuesday morning saw Thomson continue to impose himself on the Warwickshire batsmen and bring his match total to 15 wickets for 75 runs. Only on two occasions in Sussex's more recent history had a bowler taken 15 wickets in a match – Robin Marlar doing so against Glamorgan in 1952 and against Lancashire in 1955. Whatever Thomson's skill, the Midland side had done tolerably well to leave Sussex 206 to win the match. They failed abjectly. Wickets went down like ninepins to the seam of David Brown and Jack Bannister, and their innings total of 23 made in fifty-five minutes was their lowest for 42 years, Yorkshire having dismissed them for 20 at Hull in 1922. An interesting vignette associated with this match

Ian Thomson (right) with Jim Parks.

SUSSEX COUNTY CRICKET CLUB

6D.

SUSSEX
-v-
WARWICKSHIRE
Worthing Week.
June 6th, 8th & 9th. 1964

Hours of Play :-
1st day 11.30 - 7.00
2nd day 11.00 - 7.00
3rd day 11.00 - 4 or 4.30

LUNCH 1-30 to 2-10
TEA INTERVAL 20 Minutes

SUSSEX		1st Innings		2nd Innings	
1.	K.G. Suttle	c Smith(M) b Brown	33	c H. itchcock b Brown	8
2.	R.J.Langridge	c Smith (M) b Bannister	0	c Smith (M) b Bannister	1
3.	L.J. Lenham	c Ibbadulla b Bannister	2	lbw b Bannister	6
4.	† A.S.M. Oakman	c Brown b Cartwright	10	c & b Cannister	0
5.	G.C. Cooper	c Hitchcock b Brown	7	c Ibbadulla b Bannister	2
6.	F.R. Pountain	b Cartwright	3	b Brown	0
7.	N.I. Thomson	c Smith (M) b Cartwright	8	c Brown b Bannister	4
8.	A . Buss	c & b Brown	3	b Bannister	0
9.	J. Snow	Not out	21	c Barber b Cartwright	2
10.	R.V. Bell	Run out	25	Not out	0
11.	* T. Gunn	lbw b Brown	0	b Cartwright	0
		b 8 lb wd nb Extras	8	b lb wd nb Extras	
		TOTAL	120	TOTAL	23

Runs at fall of wicket	1	2	3	4	5	6	7	8	9	10
1st Innings	1	25	50	50	60	62	68	80	119	120
2nd Innings	1	15	15	15	17	17	21	21	23	23

Bowling analysis:	O	M	R	W	WB	NB	O	M	R	W	WB	NB
Brown	16/5	4	50	4	-	-	6	3	7	2	-	-
Bannister	15	7	26	2	-	-	6	2	16	6	-	-
Cartwright	26	11	36	3	-	-	0/2	-	-	2	-	-

UMPIRES: J.Arnold & A.E.Fagg.

SCORERS:
G. Washer & J.Wilkinson.

Ian Thomson all 10 wickets in Warwicks 1st Innings

† Captain
* Wicket Keeper

NEW BALL - May be claimed on completion of 85 overs.

WARWICKSHIRE		1st Innings		2nd Innings	
1.	N.F. Horner	c & b Thomson	0	c Pountain b Thomson	11
2.	R.W. Barber	c Suttle b Thomson	57	c Gunn b Buss (A)	15
3.	K. Ibadulla	c Buss b Thomson	17	lbw b Thomson	0
4.	† M.J.K. Smith	lbw b Thomson	42	st. Gunn b Buss (A)	19
5.	J.A. Jameson	b Thomson	7	c Buss (A) b Thomson	16
6.	T.W.Cartwright	st. Gunn b Thomson	54	c Cooper b Snow (J)	24
7.	R.E.Hitchcock	lbw b Thomson	2	c Bell b Buss (A)	0
8.	* A.C. Smith	b Thomson	2	c & b Snow (J)	7
9.	J.D. Bannister	c Gunn b Thomson	1	b Thomson	0
10.	R. Miller	b Thomson	7	c Buss (A) b Thomson	0
11.	D.J. Brown	Not out	0	Not out	25
		b 2 lb 3 wd nb 2 Extras	7	b 4 lb 4 wd - nb 4 Extras	12
		TOTAL	196	TOTAL	129

At Worthing:-
Wednesday, Thursday & Friday,
June 10th, 11th &12th,

SUSSEX -v- NOTTINGHAMSHIRE

At Hove:-
Wednesday, Thursday & Friday,
June 17th, 18th & 19th,

SUSSEX -v- HAMPSHIRE

Runs at fall of wicket	1	2	3	4	5	6	7	8	9	10
1st Innings	10	48	107	122	133	151	155	163	181	196
2nd Innings	18	26	26	31	64	74	93	100	100	129

Bowling analysis:	O	M	R	W	WB	NB	O	M	R	W	WB	NB
Thomson	34/2	19	49	10	-	-	25/2	15	26	5	-	2
Buss (A)	12	1	42	0	-	1	18	6	58	3	-	-
Snow (J)	16	2	52	0	-	-	7	1	33	2	-	2
Bell	11	3	35	0	-	-						
Oakman	5	2	11	0	-	-						

Ian Thomson

WARWICKSHIRE WON
182 RUNS.

SPECTATORS are requested to remain seated during the delivery of an over.

THIS card does not necessarily include the fall of the last wicket.

WARWICKSHIRE won the toss and elected to bat.

LATEST SCORE PLEASE RING - HOVE 772766

is what happened after the defeat by Yorkshire. Arthur Gilligan, then the County's captain, was so dissatisfied with his team's performance that he ordered extra net practice. It was during this session that Maurice Tate, previously an off-spinner of moderate quality, was found to be able to bowl at medium pace, a speed at which he became for at least ten years one of the world's leading bowlers.

For Sussex it was not all loss, however. In the second game of the Worthing week the County, reinforced by the return of Ted Dexter and Jim Parks from the First Test against Australia, comprehensively defeated Nottinghamshire and Thomson, with a match analysis of 8 wickets for 55, brought his weekly total to 23 wickets at less than 6 runs each. A worthy successor, of course, to Maurice Tate!

Sussex *v.* Leicestershire

14, 16 and 17 May 1966 County Championship
Leicester

Ken Suttle was in his benefit year and only six years off his retirement when he completed one of the most amazing solo performances of the post-war years in Sussex's match with Leicestershire in 1966.

Leicestershire, then captained by former Surrey and England left-arm spinner, Tony Lock, won the toss and decided to bat. Openers Maurice Hallam and Brian Booth put on 124 for the first wicket before Suttle caught and bowled Booth. Although Mick Norman and, later in the order, Tony Lock all made runs, the Leicestershire total was only par for the course. When Sussex's turn to bat came, they fared badly against the spin of Lock, John Savage and Jack Birkenshaw – every man jack an import from another county – and found themselves with a deficit of 105 runs. Only Suttle, opening the innings, batting determinedly for three hours and forty-five minutes and reaching the boundary on five occasions, showed how to play the home team's spinners, and his innings represented way over half the Sussex total.

When Leicestershire went in again, it was the turn of the Sussex spinners to show their mettle, and Alan Oakman's off-spin put a stranglehold on their batting. Sussex were left to reach 265 to win in four hours and thirty-five minutes – a not inconsiderable total in the context of the match. Suttle, partnered by Les Lenham at the top of the order, put on 94 for the first wicket and he was then joined by Richard Langridge in a second-wicket stand of 146 which took the game away from the hosts. Suttle's 139* with 1 six and 9 fours, completed ten minutes before the scheduled close, meant that he had made 228 runs without being dismissed, had taken 3 wickets and a catch, and had been on the field of play throughout the three days of the match – a wholly rare achievement for any first-class cricketer.

Ken Suttle went on the MCC tour to West Indies in 1953/54, but never attained Test match selection. He was, however, the model County professional, and only John Langridge has scored more than his total of 29,375 runs for Sussex. When he turned up to play in 1971, he was suddenly told that he was no longer required and, although he did play a few games in that season, he was consigned to the Second XI for the rest of his contract in 1972. It was a quite unworthy finish to the first-class career of a wholly worthy and dedicated cricketer.

Alan Oakman's off-spin strangled the Leicester batting.

Ken Suttle – on the field for the whole match.

Leicestershire won the toss and elected to bat

LEICESTERSHIRE				
M.R. Hallam	c M.A.Buss b Oakman	64	b Oakman	18
B.J. Booth	c and b Suttle	55	c Pataudi b Oakman	30
M.E. Norman	not out	47	b Oakman	2
P. Marner	c Bates b Suttle	2	b Suttle	35
C.C. Inman	c Lenham b Oakman	12	c Parks b A.Buss	34
J. Birkenshaw	c Langridge b Snow	17	run out	11
D. Constant	b A.Buss	5	c Parks b Snow	16
#R.W. Tolchard	b Snow	0	not out	3
*G.A.R. Lock	c Oakman b Snow	56	b Oakman	1
C.T. Spencer	c Lenham b Snow	0	c Langridge b Oakman	5
J.S. Savage	b A.Buss	2	b Oakman	0
Extras	(b6)	6	(b2, lb2)	4
TOTAL		266		159

1/124,2/124,3/127,4/156,5/189,6/200,7/201,8/263, 9/263

1/24,2/32,3/79,4/119,5/123, 6/126,7/132,8/155,9/156

Bowling	O	M	R	W	O	M	R	W
Snow	23	7	63	4	10	5	7	1
A. Buss	21.5	5	65	2	8	2	18	1
Oakman	30	9	60	2	29.5	2	94	6
M.A. Buss	16	7	23	0	5	3	5	0
Bates	4	0	13	0				
Suttle	33	16	36	2	10	1	31	1

SUSSEX				
L.J. Lenham	c Inman b Lock	10	b Lock	43
K.G. Suttle	not out	89	not out	139
R.J. Langridge	lbw b Lock	3	run out	68
#J.M. Parks	c Marner b Birkenshaw	31	not out	12
*Nawab of Pataudi	c Spencer b Birkenshaw	7		
A.S.M. Oakman	c Lock b Birkenshaw	7		
M.G. Griffith	c Tolchard b Lock	6		
M.A. Buss	c Marner b Savage	2		
A. Buss	c Lock b Savage	0		
D.L. Bates	run out	1		
J.A. Snow	b Savage	2		
Extras	(lb3)	3	(b1, lb2)	3
TOTAL		161	(for 2 wkts)	265

1/31,2/38,3/72,4/87,5/110,6/133,7/152,8/152,9/155

1/94,2/240

Bowling	O	M	R	W	O	M	R	W
Spencer	4	1	16	0	11	1	50	0
Marner	5	2	10	0	10.4	1	28	0
Lock	24	4	40	3	28	9	54	1
Savage	17.2	4	37	3	29	6	74	0
Birkenshaw	26	5	55	3	19	3	56	0

Umpires: C.S. Elliott and A.E. Rhodes

Sussex won by 8 wickets

SUSSEX *v.* AUSTRALIANS

22, 24 and 25 July 1972 Tourist Match
Hove

For a County side that has a relatively modest record in the Championship, Sussex has sometimes done particularly well against visiting Australian sides. In 1888, the visitors had succumbed to the lobs of Walter Humphreys, while in 1938, Hugh Bartlett's two-hour 157 had created a situation from which the Australians had been lucky to extricate themselves. Thirty-four years later, the County became the first County side to defeat the 1972 Australians.

Although Dennis Lillee and Bob Massie were absent, the remainder of their side was that which took on England in the Fourth Test at Leeds some two days later. Mike Griffith, on winning the toss, put the Australians in and the home bowlers, particularly Mike Buss and Tony Greig, bowled so well that the visitors' 294 was certainly below par for them. Sussex responded vigorously, Peter Graves and Geoff Greenidge posting the first 100 opening partnership against the touring team, and Greig taking 3 sixes off 1 over by Jeff Hammond and reaching 36 in only nineteen minutes. With only 5 wickets down, Griffith declared as soon as the County were in the lead. Geoff Greenidge, many thought, might well have reached his hundred, but his own nervousness in the 90s and the visitors' usual exploitation of it meant that he was caught behind one short of the magic figure.

In their second innings, the Australians batted with much greater panache in front of a crowd of more than 4,000, including the eighty-two-year-old Ted Bowley, a mainstay of Sussex inter-war batting. Keith Stackpole was in tremendous form and moved from his overnight 35 to 135 in two-and-a-half hours before lunch on the last morning. When Ian Chappell declared after lunch, the sun was still beating down and the wicket still full of runs. Some might have thought that setting a County side 261 to win in approximately three hours was an easy proposition. Others took the view that 260 runs off roughly 55 overs against a successful international side could never be easy.

Whatever the arguments, Sussex accepted the challenge. Greenidge and Graves began with a second century partnership, reaching 108 after only 88 minutes. The former and Roger Prideaux then took the score to 161 for 1 when the last 20 overs were called. One hundred runs off 20 overs seemed to be a nice round statistic and was a test of the County's ability to show the discipline required. When Prideaux was stumped at 197, a vital 89 runs had been added in forty-nine minutes and, although some wickets went down quickly in the middle order, Greenidge this time did not fail to reach his ton and, going to town against a fading attack, he and Griffith took 13 runs off the fifteenth over and the skipper made the winning hit off the second ball of the 18th. One hundred runs had come in exactly the hour. It was a truly fine win.

Geoff Greenidge – 99 in the first innings and a century in the second.

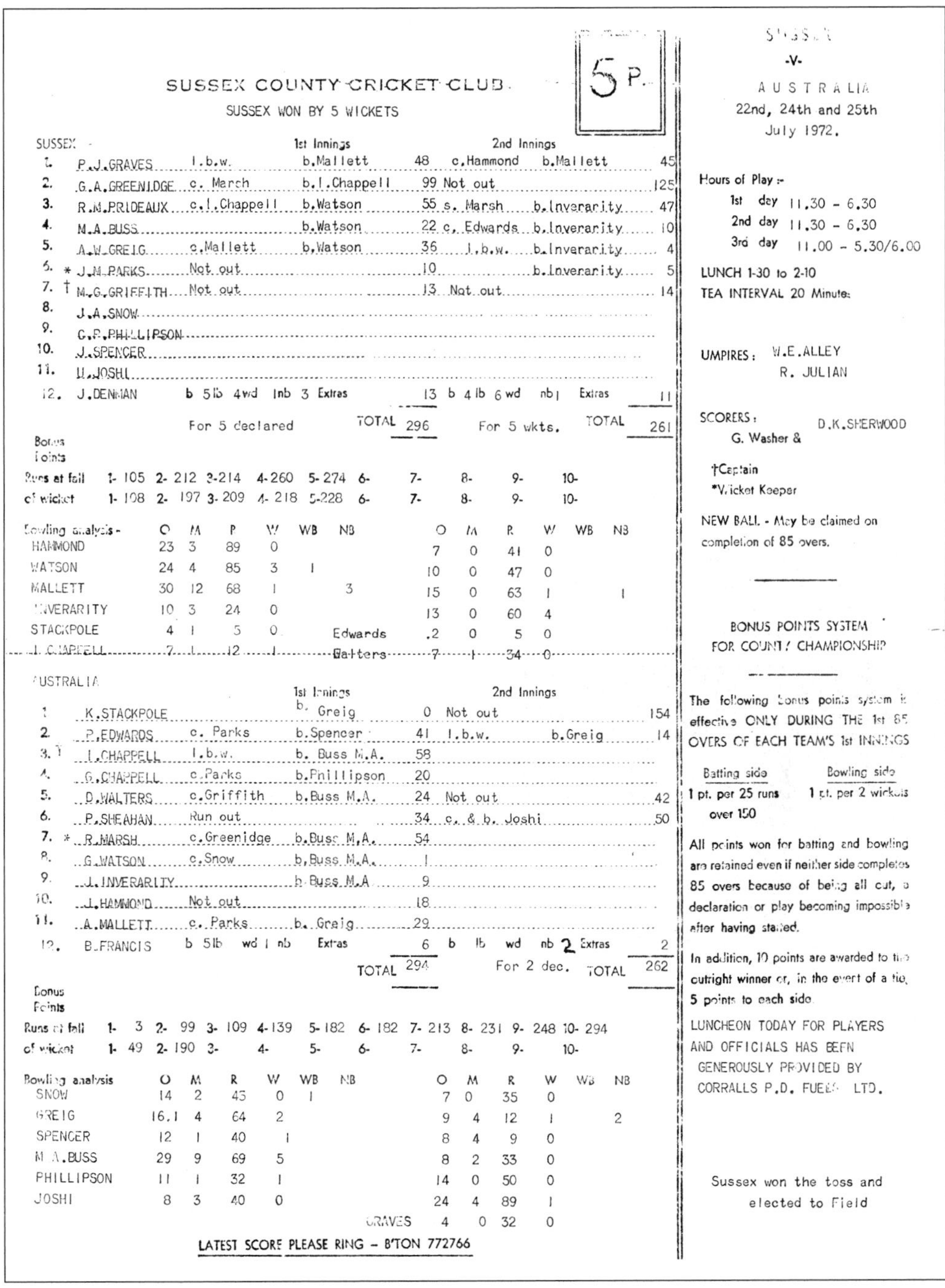

5 P.

SUSSEX COUNTY CRICKET CLUB

SUSSEX WON BY 5 WICKETS

SUSSEX

			1st Innings			2nd Innings	
1.	P.J.GRAVES	l.b.w.	b.Mallett	48	c.Hammond	b.Mallett	45
2.	G.A.GREENIDGE	c. Marsh	b.I.Chappell	99	Not out		125
3.	R.M.PRIDEAUX	c.I.Chappell	b.Watson	55	s. Marsh	b.Inverarity	47
4.	M.A.BUSS		b.Watson	22	c. Edwards	b.Inverarity	10
5.	A.W.GREIG	c.Mallett	b.Watson	36	l.b.w.	b.Inverarity	4
6.	* J.M.PARKS	Not out		10		b.Inverarity	5
7.	† M.G.GRIFFITH	Not out		13	Not out		14
8.	J.A.SNOW						
9.	C.P.PHILLIPSON						
10.	J.SPENCER						
11.	U.JOSHI						
12.	J.DENMAN	b 5lb 4wd Inb 3	Extras	13	b 4 lb 6 wd nb 1	Extras	11
		For 5 declared	TOTAL	296	For 5 wkts.	TOTAL	261

Bonus Points

Runs at fall of wicket	1-	2-	3-	4-	5-	6-	7-	8-	9-	10-
1st Innings	105	212	214	260	274					
2nd Innings	108	197	209	218	228					

Bowling analysis -	O	M	R	W	WB	NB		O	M	R	W	WB	NB
HAMMOND	23	3	89	0				7	0	41	0		
WATSON	24	4	85	3	1			10	0	47	0		
MALLETT	30	12	68	1		3		15	0	63	1		1
INVERARITY	10	3	24	0				13	0	60	4		
STACKPOLE	4	1	5	0			Edwards	.2	0	5	0		
I. CHAPPELL	7	1	12	1			Walters	7	1	34	0		

AUSTRALIA

			1st Innings			2nd Innings	
1.	K.STACKPOLE		b. Greig	0	Not out		154
2.	P.EDWARDS	c. Parks	b.Spencer	41	l.b.w.	b.Greig	14
3. †	I.CHAPPELL	l.b.w.	b. Buss M.A.	58			
4.	G.CHAPPELL	c.Parks	b.Phillipson	20			
5.	D.WALTERS	c.Griffith	b.Buss M.A.	24	Not out		42
6.	P.SHEAHAN	Run out		34	c. & b. Joshi		50
7. *	R.MARSH	c.Greenidge	b.Buss M.A.	54			
8.	G.WATSON	c.Snow	b.Buss M.A.	1			
9.	J.INVERARITY		b Buss M.A	9			
10.	J.HAMMOND	Not out		18			
11.	A.MALLETT	c. Parks	b. Greig	29			
12.	B.FRANCIS	b 5lb wd 1 nb	Extras	6	b lb wd nb 2	Extras	2
			TOTAL	294	For 2 dec.	TOTAL	262

Bonus Points

Runs at fall of wicket	1-	2-	3-	4-	5-	6-	7-	8-	9-	10-
1st Innings	3	99	109	139	182	182	213	231	248	294
2nd Innings	49	190								

Bowling analysis	O	M	R	W	WB	NB		O	M	R	W	WB	NB
SNOW	14	2	43	0	1			7	0	35	0		
GREIG	16.1	4	64	2				9	4	12	1		2
SPENCER	12	1	40	1				8	4	9	0		
M.A.BUSS	29	9	69	5				8	2	33	0		
PHILLIPSON	11	1	32	1				14	0	50	0		
JOSHI	8	3	40	0				24	4	89	1		
							GRAVES	4	0	32	0		

LATEST SCORE PLEASE RING – B'TON 772766

SUSSEX
-V-
AUSTRALIA
22nd, 24th and 25th
July 1972.

Hours of Play :-
1st day 11.30 – 6.30
2nd day 11.30 – 6.30
3rd day 11.00 – 5.30/6.00

LUNCH 1-30 to 2-10
TEA INTERVAL 20 Minutes

UMPIRES : W.E.ALLEY
R. JULIAN

SCORERS : G. Washer & D.K.SHERWOOD

†Captain
*Wicket Keeper

NEW BALL – May be claimed on completion of 85 overs.

BONUS POINTS SYSTEM FOR COUNTY CHAMPIONSHIP

The following bonus points system is effective ONLY DURING THE 1st 85 OVERS OF EACH TEAM'S 1st INNINGS

Batting side	Bowling side
1 pt. per 25 runs over 150	1 pt. per 2 wickets

All points won for batting and bowling are retained even if neither side completes 85 overs because of being all out, a declaration or play becoming impossible after having started.

In addition, 10 points are awarded to the outright winner or, in the event of a tie, 5 points to each side.

LUNCHEON TODAY FOR PLAYERS AND OFFICIALS HAS BEEN GENEROUSLY PROVIDED BY CORRALLS P.D. FUELS LTD.

Sussex won the toss and elected to Field

Sussex v. Surrey

12, 14 and 15 August 1972 — County Championship
Eastbourne

If ever Sussex threw away a virtually assured win then it occurred in the match with Surrey at the Saffrons in 1972. Only 13 overs were bowled on the first day of the match and it needed some ingenuity on the part of captains Micky Stewart and Mike Griffith to bring some life into the contest.

At the end of the Saturday, the first day, Surrey were on 38 for 1 wicket, but 372 runs were scored on the Monday as Surrey declared on 300 for 4 from 82.5 overs, and Sussex responded with 110 for 3 off 41 overs. The County's reply was sustained by Peter Graves and Roger Prideaux, who was exactly 50* at the close.

Two interesting declarations set the game alight on the Tuesday when 448 runs were scored. Prideaux, supported by Jim Parks and the skipper, reached his ton, when Sussex declared 74 runs in arrears. The Surrey batsmen then hit hard for 34 overs before Stewart made the third declaration of the match, leaving the hosts to score 205 in 135 minutes – a fairly sporting offer. At the end of the seventeenth of the compulsory last 20 overs, Sussex were cruising to victory with Prideaux, again in magnificent form, on 92 and the West Indian Geoff Greenidge on 68. It seemed highly unlikely that 18 runs could not be scored off the last 3 overs.

There then followed one of the most remarkable collapses in cricket. At this point, Pat Pocock, the Surrey and England off-spinner, when he came to bowl the eighteenth over, was enjoying an analysis of no wicket for 63 runs. With his first ball, he bowled Greenidge for 68 and Sussex were 187 for 2. The third ball bowled Mike Buss and Sussex had not moved on. Jim Parks took 2 from the fourth ball and was caught and bowled by Pocock off the last: 189 for 4. This meant that 16 runs were now required from 2 overs – not such a good situation as it was an over previously, but still manageable. The nineteenth over was bowled by Robin Jackman: Prideaux took a four and a single off the first two balls and Griffith hit the fifth ball over the boundary for six. At 200 for 4, Sussex were still well placed, requiring 5 runs from the last over, with Prideaux on strike and 97 to his name.

Pocock then came to bowl the final over, which produced several world records. Prideaux attempted to hit the first ball for six and thus end the match in one blow, but he miscalculated and was caught by Jackman on the boundary. The batsmen had crossed while the ball was in the air, so Griffith was now on strike. The second ball had him caught by Roy Lewis and the third had Jerry Morley stumped by Arnold Long, giving the bowler a hat-trick. John Spencer, coming in at number eight, took a single off the fourth ball and Tony Buss, the number nine, was bowled by the fifth and Sussex were 201 for 8. When Uday Joshi came in to take the last ball of the match, he struck it firmly, but in going for a second run he failed to make his ground and was run out. Sussex, at 202 for 9, were still 3 runs short of victory and the game was a draw.

Pocock, in his astonishing spell, had bowled seven consecutive balls at seven different batsmen. He had taken 5 wickets in 6 balls (equalling the world record) and 7 wickets in 11 balls (creating a world record), his

Peter Graves.

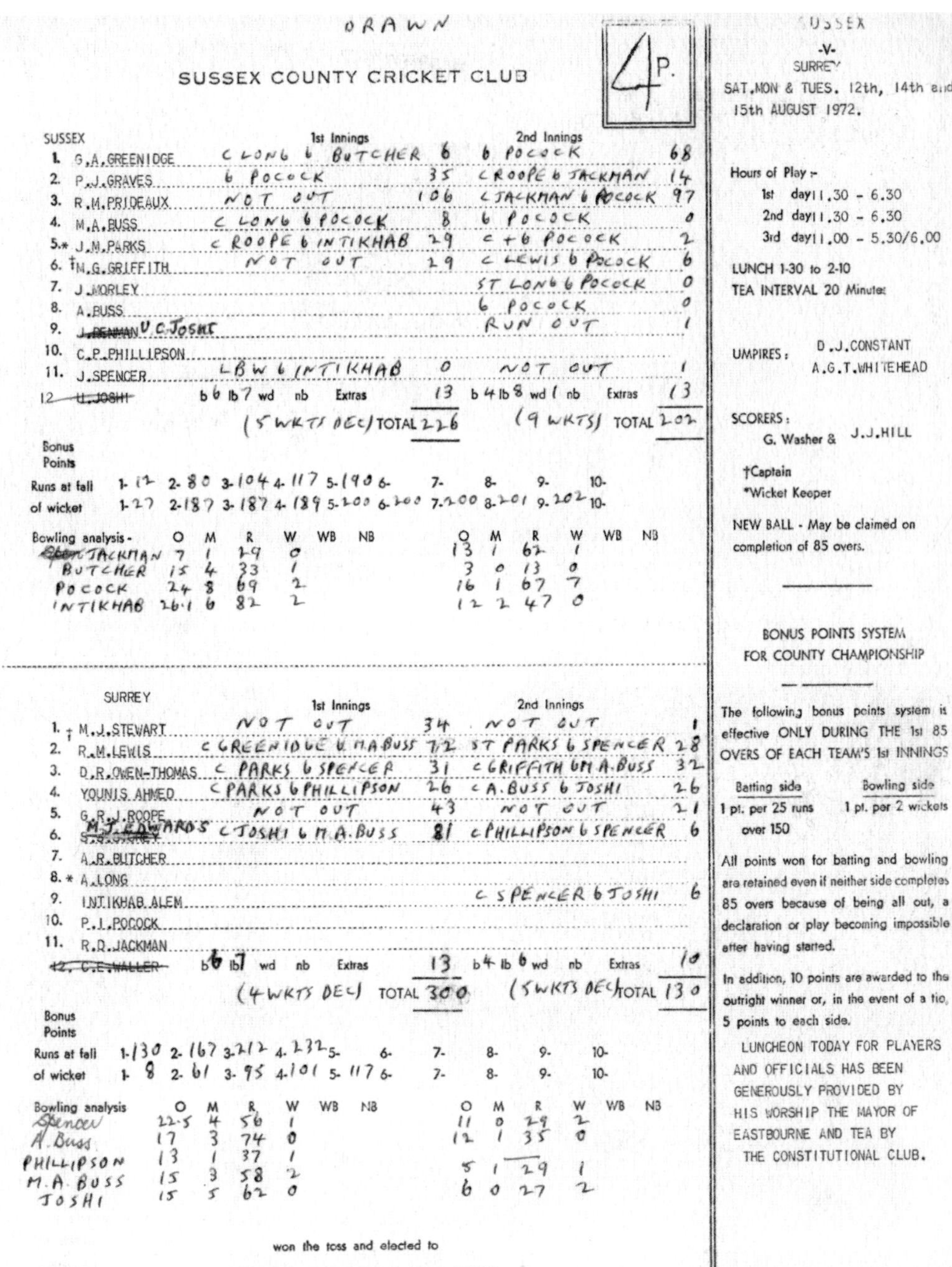

DRAWN

SUSSEX COUNTY CRICKET CLUB

4P.

SUSSEX
-V-
SURREY
SAT.MON & TUES. 12th, 14th and 15th AUGUST 1972.

	SUSSEX	1st Innings		2nd Innings	
1.	G.A.GREENIDGE	c Long b Butcher	6	b Pocock	68
2.	P.J.GRAVES	b Pocock	35	c Roope b Jackman	14
3.	R.M.PRIDEAUX	Not out	106	c Jackman b Pocock	97
4.	M.A.BUSS	c Long b Pocock	8	b Pocock	0
5.*	J.M.PARKS	c Roope b Intikhab	29	c + b Pocock	2
6. †	M.G.GRIFFITH	Not out	29	c Lewis b Pocock	6
7.	J.MORLEY			st Long b Pocock	0
8.	A.BUSS			b Pocock	0
9.	~~J.DENMAN~~ U C.JOSHI			Run out	1
10.	C.P.PHILLIPSON				
11.	J.SPENCER	lbw b Intikhab	0	Not out	1
12	~~U.JOSHI~~	b 6 lb 7 wd nb Extras	13	b 4 lb 8 wd 1 nb Extras	13
		(5 wkts dec) TOTAL	226	(9 wkts) TOTAL	202

Bonus Points

Runs at fall of wicket 1-12 2-80 3-104 4-117 5-190 6- 7- 8- 9- 10-

1-27 2-187 3-187 4-189 5-200 6-200 7-200 8-201 9-202 10-

Bowling analysis -	O	M	R	W	WB	NB	O	M	R	W	WB	NB
Jackman	7	1	29	0			13	1	62	1		
Butcher	15	4	33	1			3	0	13	0		
Pocock	24	8	69	2			16	1	67	7		
Intikhab	26.1	6	82	2			12	2	47	0		

	SURREY	1st Innings		2nd Innings	
1. †	M.J.STEWART	Not out	34	Not out	1
2.	R.M.LEWIS	c Greenidge b M.A.Buss	72	st Parks b Spencer	28
3.	D.R.OWEN-THOMAS	c Parks b Spencer	31	c Griffith b M.A.Buss	32
4.	YOUNIS AHMED	c Parks b Phillipson	26	c A.Buss b Joshi	26
5.	G.R.J.ROOPE	Not out	43	Not out	21
6.	~~S.J.STOREY~~ M.J.EDWARDS	c Joshi b M.A.Buss	81	c Phillipson b Spencer	6
7.	A.R.BUTCHER				
8. *	A.LONG				
9.	INTIKHAB ALEM			c Spencer b Joshi	6
10.	P.I.POCOCK				
11.	R.D.JACKMAN				
~~12.~~	~~C.E.WALLER~~	b 6 lb 7 wd nb Extras	13	b 4 lb 6 wd nb Extras	10
		(4 wkts dec) TOTAL	300	(5 wkts dec) TOTAL	130

Bonus Points

Runs at fall of wicket 1-130 2-167 3-212 4-232 5- 6- 7- 8- 9- 10-

1-8 2-61 3-95 4-101 5-117 6- 7- 8- 9- 10-

Bowling analysis	O	M	R	W	WB	NB	O	M	R	W	WB	NB
Spencer	22.5	4	56	1			11	0	29	2		
A.Buss	17	3	74	0			12	1	35	0		
Phillipson	13	1	37	1								
M.A.Buss	15	3	58	2			5	1	29	1		
Joshi	15	5	62	0			6	0	27	2		

won the toss and elected to

LATEST SCORE PLEASE RING – B'TON 772766

Hours of Play –
1st day 11.30 – 6.30
2nd day 11.30 – 6.30
3rd day 11.00 – 5.30/6.00

LUNCH 1-30 to 2-10
TEA INTERVAL 20 Minutes

UMPIRES: D.J.CONSTANT, A.G.T.WHITEHEAD

SCORERS: G. Washer & J.J.HILL

†Captain
*Wicket Keeper

NEW BALL - May be claimed on completion of 85 overs.

BONUS POINTS SYSTEM FOR COUNTY CHAMPIONSHIP

The following bonus points system is effective ONLY DURING THE 1st 85 OVERS OF EACH TEAM'S 1st INNINGS

Batting side	Bowling side
1 pt. per 25 runs over 150	1 pt. per 2 wickets

All points won for batting and bowling are retained even if neither side completes 85 overs because of being all out, a declaration or play becoming impossible after having started.

In addition, 10 points are awarded to the outright winner or, in the event of a tie, 5 points to each side.

LUNCHEON TODAY FOR PLAYERS AND OFFICIALS HAS BEEN GENEROUSLY PROVIDED BY HIS WORSHIP THE MAYOR OF EASTBOURNE AND TEA BY THE CONSTITUTIONAL CLUB.

last over reading WWW1W1 (run out). Sussex had lost 8 wickets in the last 3 overs while scoring 15 runs and Pocock's last 2 overs read 2-0-4-7, turning an unattractive 14-1-63-0 into an improbable 16-1-67-7.

There are no Man of the Match awards in County games, but had there been one, Pocock would surely have won it. Yet Roger Prideaux, had things eventuated differently, might have been the hero with two hundreds in the one match.

Pat Pocock – 7 wickets in 11 balls.

Roger Prideaux – close to a second hundred in his second innings.

SUSSEX v. SOMERSET

2 September 1978 Gillette Final
Lord's

Sussex had, by 1978, carved out something of a name for themselves in Gillette Cup cricket. They had won the inaugural match in 1963, had retained it in the following year, when Ian Thomson's bowling had so dominated Warwickshire that the game was done and dusted by mid-afternoon, and in 1968, 1970 and 1973, they had played well enough to reach the final. Only Lancashire, with four wins and one other final appearance, had done better than Sussex by 1978, and in this year the County went ahead in the race by reaching a sixth final. Their opponents, Somerset, boasted the strength of Ian Botham and the two West Indian stars, Viv Richards and Joel Garner, the latter arguably as effective a West Indian fast-bowler as any after Malcolm Marshall. Somerset had raced through to the final, although they beat Essex in the semi-finals only by losing fewer wickets, whereas Sussex had experienced the odd hiccup, beating minor county Staffordshire by 2 runs and winning against Yorkshire only as the result of an unpredictable 10-over slog. Without doubt, Sussex came to Lord's as the underdogs.

Arnold Long, who had become captain only in this year, won the toss and, after some deliberation, decided to put the strong Somerset side in to bat. It was a bold and courageous decision, based largely on the fact that there was going to be some moisture in the pitch but, when Imran's first over went for 14 runs – a Somerset wag commented that his side was on course for a total of 840 at that rate of scoring – it looked perhaps as if he had miscalculated. But he was not wrong – it was the crucial tactical decision of the match. Geoff Arnold conceded 7 runs from 6 overs and, when Imran knocked over Denning's off-stump, things were beginning to get back on course. A double change brought on Giles Cheatle's slow left-arm and John Spencer's miserly medium-pace, and even the great Viv Richards, seemed a touch restricted. By lunchtime, he had been caught at deep square-leg off John Barclay's superbly controlled off-spin. The combative Botham, of course, sought to make a fight out of it, hitting Arnold for a fine six, which few would have attempted and even fewer accomplished. When he was out, however, bowled neck and crop by Imran, the Somerset innings seemed to peter out at 207 for 7 wickets.

Despite facing an attack containing Garner and Botham, Sussex were at this stage well-placed, but by no means favourites to win, except perhaps in the minds of the many Sussex fans. Barclay and Gehan Mendis, however, produced precisely the sound start that was needed, and added 93 before they were parted. When they both had gone, however, and Sussex's middle-order powerhouse of Javed Miandad and Imran had made 3 runs between them, the score stood at 110 for 4. Somerset appeared to be on the way back. Rose, the

John Barclay scores a boundary off Dredge.

THE
Gillette Cup 1978

Winners receive £5,000 Runners-Up £2,000

'Man of the Match' in each round receives £100, a Gold Medal valued at £140 and a 'Man of the Match' Winners Tie

MARYLEBONE CRICKET CLUB

Gillette Cup Final

10p **SOMERSET v. SUSSEX** 10p

at Lord's Ground, †Saturday, September 2nd, 1978

Any alterations to teams will be announced over the loud speaker system

SOMERSET		
‡1 B. C. Rose	c Long b Cheatle	30
2 P. W. Denning	b Imran	0
3 I. V. A. Richards	c Arnold b Barclay	44
4 P. M. Roebuck	c Mendis b Cheatle	9
5 I. T. Botham	b Imran	80
6 V. J. Marks	c Arnold b Barclay	4
*7 D. J. S. Taylor	not out	13
8 G. I. Burgess	run out	3
9 K. F. Jennings		
10 C. H. Dredge		
11 J. Garner	not out	8
	B , l-b 10 , w , n-b 6 ,	16
60 overs	(7 wkts) Total...	207

FALL OF THE WICKETS

1—22 2—53 3—73 4—115 5—151 6—157 7—194 8— 9— 10—

Bowling Analysis	O.	M.	R.	W.	Wd.	N-b
Imran	12	1	50	2	...	...
Arnold	12	2	43	0	...	...
Spencer	12	3	27	0	...	...
Cheatle	12	3	56	2	...	...
Barclay	12	3	21	2	...	...

SUSSEX		
1 J. R. T. Barclay	c Roebuck b Botham	44
2 G. D. Mendis	c Marks b Burgess	44
3 P. W. G. Parker	not out	62
4 Javed Miandad	c Taylor b Garner	0
5 Imran Khan	c and b Botham	3
6 C. P. Phillipson	c Taylor b Dredge	32
7 S. J. Storey	not out	0
‡*8 A. Long		
9 J. Spencer		
10 G. G. Arnold		
11 R. G. L. Cheatle		
	B , l-b , w , n-b ,	...
53.1 overs	(5 wkts) Total...	211

FALL OF THE WICKETS

1—93 2—106 3—106 4—110 5—207 6— 7— 8— 9— 10—

Bowling Analysis	O.	M.	R.	W.	Wd.	N-b
Garner	12	3	34	1	...	...
Dredge	10	2	26	1	...	...
Botham	12	1	65	2	...	...
Jennings	9	1	29	0	...	...
Burgess	10	2	27	1	...	...
Denning	0.1	0	4	0	...	...

RULES—1 The Match will consist of one innings per side and each innings is limited to 60 overs.
2 No one bowler may bowl more than 12 overs in an innings.
3 Hours of play: 10.30 a.m. to 7.30 p.m. In certain circumstances the Umpires may order extra time.

Luncheon Interval 12.45 p.m.—1.25 p.m. Tea Interval 15 minutes (time according to state of game).

‡Captain *Wicket-keeper

Umpires—H. D. Bird & B. J. Meyer Scorers—T. Brice & G. G. A. Saulez

†This match is intended to be completed in one day, but three days have been allocated in case of weather interference

Sussex won the toss and elected to field

Sussex won by 5 wickets

Total runs scored at end of each over:-

FIRST	1	2	3	4	5	6	7	8	9	10	11	12	13	14	15	16	17	18	19	20
INNINGS	21	22	23	24	25	26	27	28	29	30	31	32	33	34	35	36	37	38	39	40
	41	42	43	44	45	46	47	48	49	50	51	52	53	54	55	56	57	58	59	60
SECOND	1	2	3	4	5	6	7	8	9	10	11	12	13	14	15	16	17	18	19	20
INNINGS	21	22	23	24	25	26	27	28	29	30	31	32	33	34	35	36	37	38	39	40
	41	42	43	44	45	46	47	48	49	50	51	52	53	54	55	56	57	58	59	60

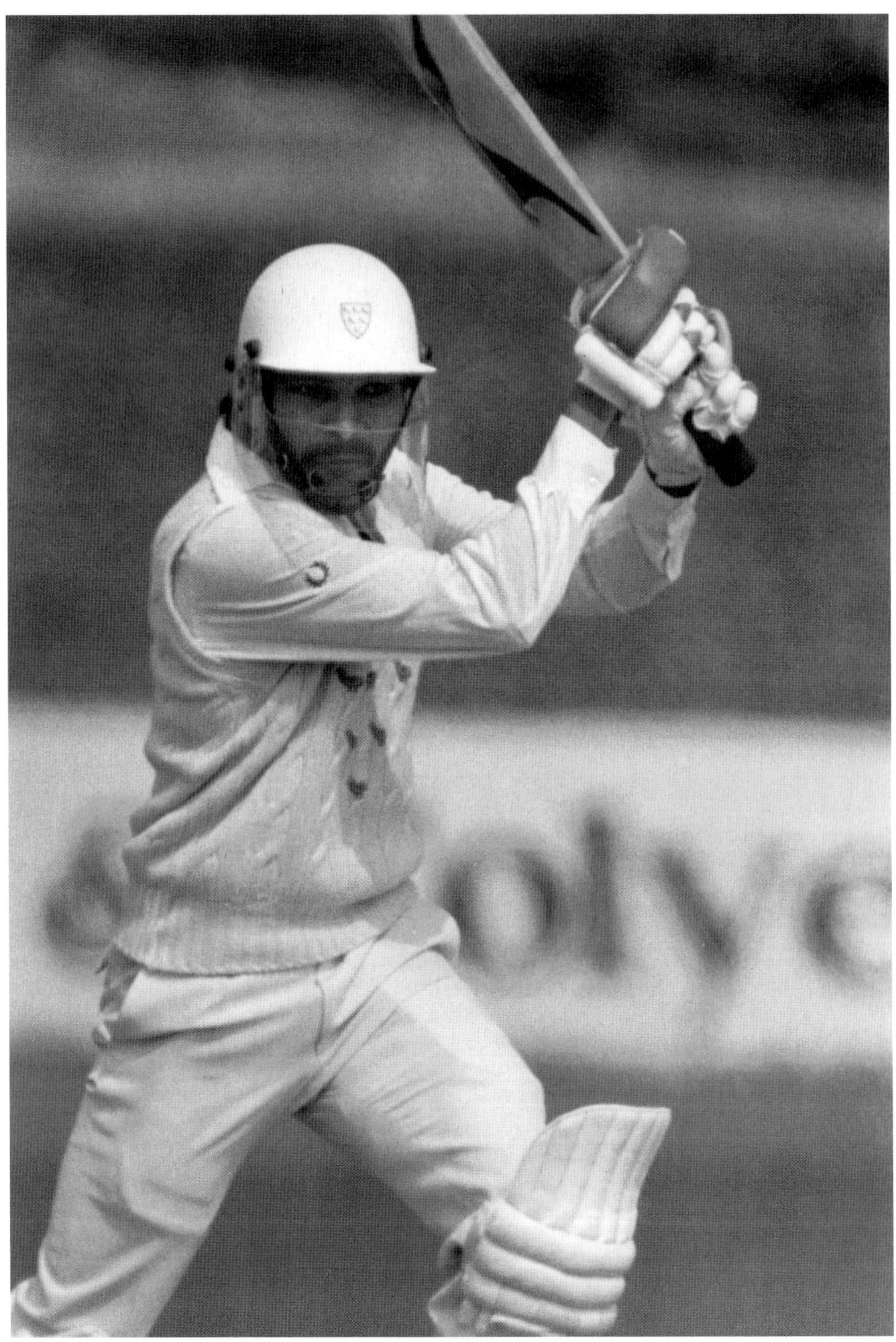

Gehan Mendis – part of a useful opening stand.

Skipper Arnold Long acknowledges the Sussex supporters.

Somerset captain, may then have made a crucial error; by taking off Garner and Botham, who might conceivably have done irretrievable harm to the Sussex innings. He allowed Paul Parker and Paul Phillipson the breathing space they needed. Had either – especially perhaps Parker – gone quickly, the game would have been up for Sussex. They met the challenge with style and panache, however, and when Phillipson went after a 97-run partnership, all Parker had to do was see the County cruise into harbour with, almost inexplicably, nearly 7 overs still to be bowled. It was not even a narrow victory: it was a comprehensive defeat for Somerset.

Paul Parker, deservedly, won the Man of the Match award, although Barclay must have been close, but the brains behind this remarkable victory was the astute Sussex skipper, Arnold Long. He had come from Surrey, where in later years he had found difficulty in holding down the 'keeper's slot and almost certainly would not have become County captain, had Tony Greig not defected to the Packer circus. As it panned out, his three years in charge represented a period of solid re-building and no little success for his adopted County, and produced a solid basis on which his successor as captain, John Barclay, built with great aplomb.

Sussex v. Derbyshire

12, 13 and 14 August 1981 County Championship
Eastbourne

The Eastbourne Cricket Week at the Saffrons in August 1981 was one of the most successful in the event, attracting over 25,000 spectators and including a controversial Sunday League match with Kent and two fine wins in the Championship over Kent and Derbyshire. It also produced some of the finest individual cricket played for Sussex in relatively recent history when Imran Khan changed what was meandering into a dull draw into a win for the County with five balls to spare.

The first half of the week, when the wicket had been rather green, had seen a thoroughly professional performance by Sussex under their new captain, John Barclay, which demolished Kent by 8 wickets. The second half of the week saw a turn in the weather. Dull and damp became hot and sunny. Derbyshire scored a competent 256 with South African, Peter Kirsten, half-brother of the now more famous Gary, playing well for his 85. Sussex responded just as competently and declared 6 runs behind. By the middle of the afternoon on the last day, Derbyshire, with only 3 second-innings wickets down, were, in the persons of Alan Hill and David Steele, playing boring cricket and patting back the leg-breaks of Colin Wells, who had forsaken his normal medium-pace in an attempt to winkle out the Derbyshire middle-order. A dull draw for the Midlanders was obviously better than risking a loss. At this point, Imran suggested to his skipper that the conditions might be ripe for him to try some reverse swing (although in 1981 that term was not perhaps in current usage on the county circuit). Although Barclay was keen to ask the umpires to exchange what was by now an extremely ragged ball, Imran was wholly against this, soon trapping David Steele lbw for 59 and, in the course of taking 4 wickets in 5 balls, blowing away the rest of the visitors' batting.

Sussex needed 234 to win in about 40 overs – a relatively tall order. Imran, feeling that this was his day, asked to be promoted to number four in the batting order, despite having been as low as seven in the first innings. Gehan Mendis went early, but a breezy second-wicket partnership of 70 between Paul Parker and Ian Gould set the County on their way. Imran entered at this point and proceeded to flay the Derbyshire attack, his fifty coming up in 36 minutes and his century in 88, as 3 sixes and 11 fours flew from his bat. Off the first ball of the last over, Sussex were home by 5 wickets and, in the course of the week, pocketed 47 Champion-ship points and second place in the table.

1981 was, of course, one of the County's most successful seasons. After a battle royal with Nottinghamshire, Sussex were pipped by 2 points. Nevertheless, it was a marvellous season for Sussex under their new captain, as they reached their highest place since the heady days of David Sheppard's leadership in 1953.

Imran Khan made a remarkable all-round display.

Derbyshire won the toss and elected to bat

DERBYSHIRE

*B. Wood	lbw b Arnold	24	lbw b Imran	12
J.G. Wright	b Greig	73	lbw b le Roux	0
P.N. Kirsten	b Greig	85	c Waller b Wells	68
D.S. Steele	b Greig	12	lbw b Imran	59
G. Miller	b Greig	0	c Phillipson b Wells	22
A. Hill	run out	5	run out	16
K.J. Barnett	c Waller b le Roux	0	b Waller	22
#R.W. Taylor	b Imran	16	not out	11
C.J. Tunnicliffe b Arnold		12	b Imran	0
P.G. Newman	not out	0	lbw b Imran	0
S. Oldham	lbw b Arnold	7	lbw b Imran	0
Extras	(b6, lb8, w2, nb6)	22	(b11, lb1, w2, nb3)	17
TOTAL		256		227

1/90,2/130,3/166,4/168,5/188,6/189,7/225,8/241,9/249 — 1/2,2/134,3/168,4/193,5/193, 6/226, 7/227,8/227,9/227

Bowling	O	M	R	W	O	M	R	W
le Roux	18	3	47	1	9	2	21	1
Arnold	21.2	6	44	3	12	4	16	0
Imran	19	4	55	1	17.1	5	52	5
Greig	22	3	75	4	5	1	20	0
Waller	6	1	13	0	26	8	46	1
Wells					17	3	55	2

SUSSEX

G.D. Mendis	c Oldham b Newman	17	lbw b Newman	1
*J.R.T. Barclay	retired hurt	37		
G.S. le Roux	c Wright b Newman	40		
P.W.G. Parker	not out	82	(3) c sub b Miller	41
I.A. Greig	lbw b Newman	0	c Newman b Miller	5
C.M. Wells	st Taylor b Steele	11	c Barnett b Miller	1
Imran Khan	c Barnett b Steele	2	(4) not out	107
C.P. Phillipson	b Newman	0	(7) not out	39
#I.J. Gould	run out	38	(2) c sub b Newman	29
G.G. Arnold	not out	2		
C.E. Waller	did not bat			
Extras	(lb2 nb19)	21	(lb3, w1, nb8)	12
TOTAL	(for 7 wkts dec.)	250	(for 5 wkts)	235

1/23,2/83,3/124,4/151,5/154,6/154,7/223 — 1/4,2/74,3/82,4/98,5/102

Bowling	O	M	R	W	O	M	R	W
Oldham	14.4	1	38	0				
Newman	20	2	73	4	14.1	2	66	2
Steele	13	3	32	2	5	0	47	0
Miller	7	3	20	0	8	0	44	3
Tunnicliffe	21	6	47	0	11	0	66	0
Wood	7.3	2	19	0				

Umpires: B.J. Meyer and R.S. Herman

Sussex won by 5 wickets

SUSSEX *v.* LANCASHIRE

6 September 1986 — NatWest Final
Lord's

Sussex came to their seventh final in the Gillette/NatWest tournament in 1986 after impressive early round performances, including an excellent quarter-final win over Yorkshire and success in a rather understated semi-final against Worcestershire. If anything they were perhaps marginal favourites, although the presence of Lancashire's captain, the great West Indian batsman, Clive Lloyd, always had the potential to make some impact on a game of cricket. In the end, as *The Cricketer*'s correspondent noted, 'the straight bats of Sussex beat the crooked bats of Lancashire by 7 wickets.' Despite there being only ten balls left when the winning run was scored, it was essentially a comfortable victory.

After Ian Gould, on winning the toss on an overcast morning, had given Lancashire first innings, it seemed as though he might have taken the wrong option. Gehan Mendis, once a Sussex player, and Graeme Fowler moved easily along to 50 in 13 overs before the latter chased a wide ball and was caught behind. Six runs later, Dermot Reeve, whose medium pace was doubtless aided by the muggy conditions, trapped Mendis lbw with the first ball of his third over. This opened the way for Lloyd, whose appearance was applauded, not least by the Sussex team, all the way to the wicket, as this was likely to be his last final at Lord's. When Reeve trapped him lbw with the fifth ball of the same over, a stunned silence – one almost of embarrassment – seemed to come across the ground. Throughout his 12 overs, Reeve bowled to a good length on the slowish pitch and was backed, as Colin Wells also was, by the Sussex skipper's attacking instinct which kept in two slips and had only two men outside the fielding circle.

At lunch, Lancashire were on 99 for 4 at exactly 3 runs per over, but after 40 overs they had slipped to 112 for 5 wickets. Then, however, Andy Hayhurst and Neil Fairbrother, who, it is said, is never happier than when he has to chase 8 runs an over, added 103 together for the sixth wicket and started to revive the fortunes of their side. Gould seemed reluctant to recall Imran Khan for a second spell, and Hayhurst,

Clive Lloyd lbw to Dermot Reeve. Ian Gould behind the wicket joins in the appeal, while Colin Wells looks on expectantly.

National Westminster Bank Trophy 1986

The County winning the Trophy will receive a prize of £19,000, the losing Finalist £9,500, the losing Semi-finalists £4,500 each and the losing Quarter-finalists £2,250 each.

MARYLEBONE CRICKET CLUB

SUSSEX WON BY 7 WICKETS

NatWest Bank Trophy Final

20p **LANCASHIRE v. SUSSEX** **20p**

at Lord's Ground, †Saturday, September 6th, 1986

LANCASHIRE		
1 G. Fowler	c GOULD b CM WELLS	24
2 G. D. Mendis	LBW b REEVE	17
3 J. Abrahams	c PIGOTT b REEVE	20
‡4 C. H. Lloyd	LBW b REEVE	0
5 N. H. Fairbrother	b PIGOTT	63
6 S. J. O'Shaughnessy	b REEVE	4
7 A. N. Hayhurst	c GOULD b IMRAN	49
*8 C. Maynard	c GOULD b IMRAN	14
9 M. Watkinson	NOT OUT	15
10 J. Simmons	NOT OUT	6
11 P. J. W. Allott		
B 1, l-b 17, w 6, n-b 6,	...	30
(8 WKTS; 60 OVERS)	Total...	242

FALL OF THE WICKETS
1...50 2...56 3...56 4...85 5...100 6...203 7...205 8...217 9... 10...

Bowling Analysis	O.	M.	R	W.	Wd.	N-b
IMRAN KHAN	12	2	43	2	...	...
LE ROUX	9	0	43	0	...	...
JONES	3	0	25	0	...	...
CM WELLS	12	3	34	1	...	...
REEVE	12	4	20	4	...	...
PIGOTT	12	1	59	1	...	...
	...	...	...	...	...	...

SUSSEX		
1 A. M. Green	ST MAYNARD b SIMMONS	62
2 R. I. Alikhan	b ALLOTT	6
3 P. W. G. Parker	c ABRAHAMS b HAYHURST	85
4 Imran Khan	NOT OUT	50
5 C. M. Wells	NOT OUT	17
6 A. P. Wells		
‡*7 I. J. Gould		
8 G. S. le Roux		
9 D. A. Reeve		
10 A. C. S. Pigott		
11 A. N. Jones		
B , l-b 17, w 6, n-b ,	...	23
(3 WKTS, 58.2 OVERS)	Total...	243

FALL OF THE WICKETS
1...19 2...156 3...190 4... 5... 6... 7... 8... 9... 10...

Bowling Analysis	O.	M.	R.	W.	Wd.	N-b
WATKINSON	11.2	0	40	0	...	...
ALLOTT	11	3	34	1	...	...
O'SHAUGHNESSY	6	0	52	0	...	...
HAYHURST	12	2	38	1	...	...
SIMMONS	12	2	31	1	...	...
ABRAHAMS	3	0	15	0	...	...
FAIRBROTHER	3	0	16	0	...	...

Any alterations to teams will be announced over the public address system

RULES—1 The Match will consist of one innings per side and each innings is limited to 60 overs.
2 No one bowler may bowl more than 12 overs in an innings.
3 Hours of play: 10.30 a.m. to 7.10 p.m. In certain circumstances the Umpires may order extra time.

Luncheon Interval 12.45 p.m.—1.25 p.m. Tea Interval will be 20 minutes and will normally be taken at 4.30 p.m.

‡Captain *Wicket-keeper

Umpires—H. D. Bird & K. E. Palmer Scorers—E. Solomon, L. V. Chandler & W. Davies

†This match is intended to be completed in one day, but three days have been allocated in case of weather interference

MAN OF MATCH: D.A. REEVE

Total runs scored at end of each over:

First Innings	1	2	3	4	5	6	7	8	9	10	11	12	13	14	15	16	17	18	19	20
	21	22	23	24	25	26	27	28	29	30	31	32	33	34	35	36	37	38	39	40
	41	42	43	44	45	46	47	48	49	50	51	52	53	54	55	56	57	58	59	60
Second Innings	1	2	3	4	5	6	7	8	9	10	11	12	13	14	15	16	17	18	19	20
	21	22	23	24	25	26	27	28	29	30	31	32	33	34	35	36	37	38	39	40
	41	42	43	44	45	46	47	48	49	50	51	52	53	54	55	56	57	58	59	60

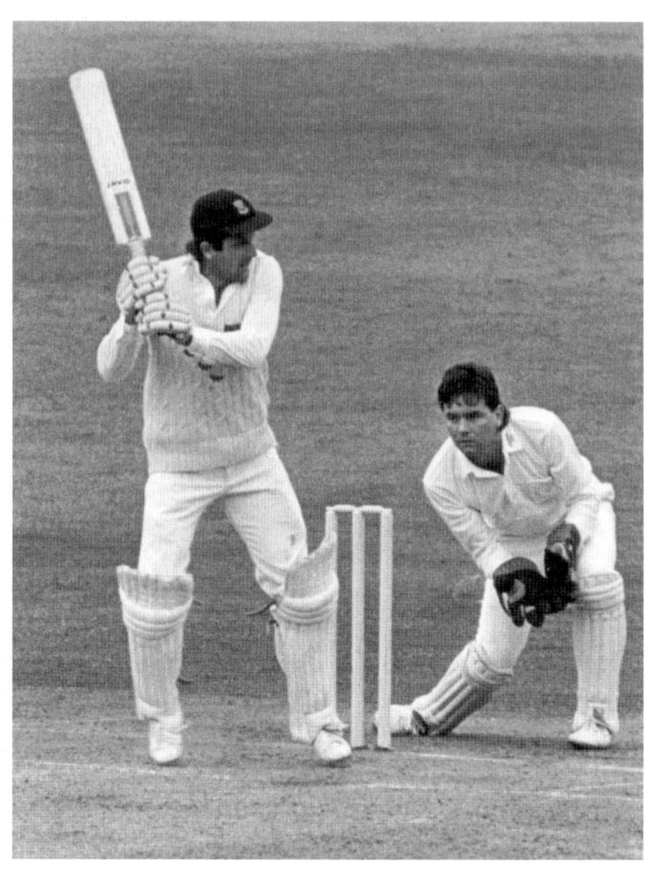

Paul Parker's innings was crucial in Sussex's victory.

Alan Green sweeps while Lancashire 'keeper Chris Maynard looks on.

Dermot Reeve receives the Man of the Match award.

defending solidly and lofting the ball when necessary, was especially severe on an out-of-form Garth le Roux. For a while Sussex lost the initiative, but when Imran came back, Hayhurst and Fairbrother were both dismissed and, although Chris Maynard took 3 successive fours off Imran and 'Winker' Watkinson hit Tony Pigott for a straight six in the last over, a total of 242 in 60 overs, albeit the fifth highest total in a one-day final, meant that Sussex had to score at a rate of only 4 runs per over.

Rehan Alikhan, looking somewhat out of his depth, left early in the County's innings, but then Alan Green, seen (wrongly) by no less a judge than John Arlott as a future England player, and Paul Parker, the recipient of a sole England cap, played immaculately straight and were shrewd enough to take the weight off a shot and run a ball to the fieldsman, both reaching their fifties before tea when Sussex were well placed at 117 for 1 wicket after 35 overs. The second-wicket stand realised 137 before Green was stumped, having received 106 balls and hit 7 fours. John Abrahams and Fairbrother were now called on to try to bolster the apparently threadbare Lancashire attack, but Sussex had by now truly mastered it and, although Parker, assailed by bouts of cramp, was finally caught at long-leg after hitting a six and 5 fours, Imran and Colin Wells calmly took control and, with ten balls still to be bowled, led their side to an impressive fourth one-day final victory.

It had been a splendid day for Sussex, and their 243 was, at the time, the highest score recorded by a side batting second in a one-day domestic final. Sir Leonard Hutton must have had difficulty in deciding on the Man of the Match award, but finally Reeve's clever bowling was rated more highly than Parker's immaculate strokeplay.

Sussex v. Hampshire

7 June 1987 Sunday League
Horsham

Although Sussex won the John Player League in 1982, they have never had the same sort of success in the shorter form of one-day cricket as they have had in matches extending to 60 overs. 1987 was rather a poor year for them – equal fourteenth place in the Refuge Assurance League – but the Hampshire match in this year was certainly what this sort of cricket is all about.

The leafy Horsham ground, overlooked by the parish church at one end and with trains passing close to the boundary at the other, is an attractive venue at all times, and the excitement generated at the end of this match was enormous. Ian Gould, on winning the toss, inserted Hampshire, the previous season's Sunday League Champions, and, although three of the visitors were out for 57, Paul Terry and Kevan James nearly doubled the score. Later on, Chris Smith and Terry added a further 63. The latter's 75 was a composed innings, and the nearest he came to losing equilibrium was when Garth le Roux, in his first over, split Terry's bat from top to bottom. Hampshire's final total gave them more than a sporting chance of victory.

Sussex appeared to be losing their way at the start of their innings, although Colin Wells' quick-fire 70 contained 2 sixes. When he holed out at deep mid-wicket, Sussex still needed 99 from 13 overs. Despite Rajesh Maru's teasing left-arm spin winkling out two members of the County's middle-order, the powerful le Roux was totally on song and hit James for successive sixes and Cardigan Connor for another. With 2 overs left, Ian Waring, Sussex's number ten, was at the wicket and 27 runs were still required. James, who bowled the penultimate over, went for 15, le Roux hitting him over mid-wicket and straight for 2 further sixes. So when Mark Nicholas, as gathering storm clouds approached the ground, called up Maru for the final over, 2 runs per ball were still needed. The first 4 balls went for 7 runs and Waring was run out off the fifth. Fortunately for Sussex, the batsmen had crossed and this enabled le Roux to get on strike and to win the match with a sixth six, his 83 having been made off a mere 54 balls.

1987 was le Roux's last season with Sussex. One of many South Africans for whom *apartheid* had meant the loss of an outstanding cricketing career, he had come to Sussex in 1978 and, when he and Imran Khan were bowling in harness, the County had the most formidable opening attack on the circuit. Imran was, of course, a class act as a batsman, but le Roux's own contribution with the bat certainly put him firmly into the all-rounder class.

Garth le Roux – a fast bowler, but also a powerful hitter.

SCORECARD

Batsman	How out	Runs
1. A.M. Green	c Parks b Tremlett	17
2. A.P. Wells	c Maru b James	10
3. C.M. Wells	c Scott b Tremlett	70
4.* I.J. Gould	b Tremlett	7
5. G.S. Le Roux	not out	83
6. D.A. Reeve	c Marshall b Maru	6
7. S.D. ~~Myles~~	b Maru	4
8.+ P. Moores	run out	0
~~9. P.A.W. Heseltine~~		
10. I.C. Waring	run out	8
11. A.M. Babington	not out	0
12. C.I.O. Ricketts	lbw b Connor	9
Extras: b: lb: 2 nb: w: 2		4
Scoring Rate: (40 overs 9 wickets)	TOTAL:	218

Bowling Analysis	1	2	3	4	5	6	7	8	O	M	R	W	nb	w
James									8	1	82	1		
Connor									8	0	42	1		
Marshall									8	0	29	0		
Tremlett									8	0	36	3		
Maru									8	1	57	2		

Fall of wickets: 1-47 2-56 3-57 4-104 5-167 6-198 7-210 8- 9-

Batsman	How out	Runs
1. V.P. Terry	c Green b C. Wells	75
2. R.J. Scott	run out	23
3. D.R. Turner	c Moores b Reeve	1
4.* M.C.J. Nicholas	lbw b Waring	1
5. C.L. Smith	c Moores b Le Roux	54
6. K.D. James	run out	31
7. M.D. Marshall	c Waring b Le Roux	7
8.+ R.J. Parks	not out	9
9. T.M. Tremlett	not out	1
10. R.J. Maru		
11. C.A. Connor		
~~12. S.J.W. Andrew~~		
Extras: b: lb: 5 nb: 4 w: 5		14
Scoring Rate: (40 overs 7 wickets)	TOTAL:	216

Bowling Analysis	1	2	3	4	5	6	7	8	O	M	R	W	nb	w
C.M. Wells									8	0	39	1		
Le Roux									8	1	46	2		
Waring									8	0	34	1		
Reeve									8	0	33	1		
Babington									6	0	42	0		
Ricketts									2	0	17	0		

Fall of wickets: 1-16 2-52 3-88 4-118 5-130 6-147 7-148 8-171 9-208

Runs per over	1	2	3	4	5	6	7	8	9	10	11	12	13	14	15	16	17	18	19	20	21	22	23	24	25	26	27	28	29	30	31	32	33	34	35	36	37	38	39	40

Sussex v. Yorkshire

9, 10 and 12 August 1991 — County Championship
Middlesbrough

Martyn Moxon must have had second thoughts about his decision to bat when Yorkshire wickets started to fall regularly in this match at Acklam Park. He had not perhaps realised that the pitch at the Green Lane end was likely to offer extra bounce and, but for some poor Sussex catching, his side would probably have been routed. As it happened, they reached a meagre 241 in face of some excellent seam bowling by Adrian Jones and Tony Dodemaide. Sussex had some batting to do at the end of the first day, and they too did not find the going easy, reaching 53 for the loss of 4 wickets by the close.

The Wells brothers, Colin and Alan, were the overnight not-out batsmen and, although they added 84 for the fifth wicket, Sussex were soon on 144 for 6 and a first-innings lead looked unlikely. Jamie Hall, batting unusually low at number eight, helped Alan Wells to add 81, but it was not until Bradleigh Donelan joined the acting captain – Paul Parker was absent owing to injury – that the innings started to take real shape, and the day closed with Sussex 115 runs on with 3 wickets still intact, with Alan Wells poised to reach his double hundred. The eighth-wicket partnership continued the following morning and reached 178 in 44 overs. Not only did it boost the County's total beyond 400, but it also broke the all-comers' record for that wicket against Yorkshire, replacing the 172 by Ewart Astill and Sussex's Arthur Gilligan, who were playing for MCC at Scarborough in 1923. When the County were finally all out, Alan

YORKSHIRE V SUSSEX

FRIDAY 9th AUGUST, SATURDAY 10th AUGUST, MONDAY 12th AUGUST 1991

YORKSHIRE C.C.C.	FIRST INNINGS	
* 1.M.D. MOXON	lbw b JONES	33
2.A.A. METCALFE	ct MOORES b DODEMAIDE	1
3.D. BYAS	ct MOORES b JONES	8
† 4. R.J. BLAKEY	ct MOORES b C.M. WELLS	33
5.P.E. ROBINSON	ct SPEIGHT b JONES	8
6.S.A. KELLETT	ct Sub b JONES	66
7.P. CARRICK	ct MOORES b JONES	2
8.C.S. PICKLES	ct SAILSBURY b DODEMAIDE	48
9.P.J. HARTLEY	ct MOORES b DODEMAIDE	17
10.J.D. BATTY	ct SMITH b DODEMAIDE	5
11.M.A. ROBINSON	NOT OUT	1
Extras	b4, 8lb, 7nb, Total 19	Total 241

Fall of Wickets: 1-8 2-27 3-82 4-95 5-161 6-191 7-203 8-229 9-240

Bowling Analysis	Overs	Mdns.	Runs	Wkts.
A.N. JONES	18	3	46	5
A.I.C. DODEMAIDE	24	2	67	4
C.M. WELLS	11	2	30	1
B.T.P. DONELAN	13	4	32	0
I.D.K. SAILSBURY	19	5	54	0

YORKSHIRE C.C.C.	SECOND INNINGS	
* 1.M.D. MOXON	C SUB B. JONES	0
2.A.A. METCALFE	C AND B DONELAN	36
3.D. BYAS	C. MOORES B DONELAN	46
† 4. R.J. BLAKEY	RUN OUT	0
5.P.E. ROBINSON	LBW B SALISBURY	10
6.S.A. KELLETT	B JONES	8
7.P. CARRICK	C. SALISBURY B. DONELAN	14
8.C.S. PICKLES	C. MOORES B. DODEMAIDE	33
9.P.J. HARTLEY	C. MOORES B JONES	10
10.J.D. BATTY	NOT OUT	1
11.M.A. ROBINSON	LBW B JONES	0
Extras	b2 lb9 nb2 TOTAL 13	Total 171

Fall of Wickets: 1 0 2 76 3 90 4 100 5 100 6 121 7 146 8 170 9 171

Bowling Analysis	Overs	Mdns.	Runs	Wkts.
A.N. JONES	12.5	2	41	4
A.I.C. DODEMAIDE	21	8	36	1
I.D.K. SALISBURY	12	4	36	1
B.T.P. DONELAN	27	15	43	3
C.M. WELLS	4	1	4	0

SUSSEX C.C.C.	FIRST INNINGS	
3 1.D.M. SMITH	b ROBINSON	11
1 2.N.J.L. LENHAM	ct BLAKEY b HARTLEY	0
8 3.J.W. HALL	C. MOXON B. CARRICK	28
* 4.A.P. WELLS	NOT OUT	253
5.M.P. SPEIGHT	ct ROBINSON b HARTLEY	7
6.C.M.WELLS	C. KELLETT B. CARRICK	42
7.A.I.C. DODEMAIDE	C. P.E. ROBINSON B. CARRICK	11
2 † 8.P. MOORES	ct P.E. ROBINSON b M.A. ROBINSON	9
10 9.I.D.K. SALISBURY	ST. BLAKEY B. CARRICK	3
9 10.B.T.P. DONELAN	RUN OUT	59
11.A.N. JONES	C. KELLETT B. CARRICK	1
Extras	b1 lb6 w1 nb4 TOTAL 12	Total 436

Fall of Wickets: 1-0 2-20 3-33 4-40 5 124 6 144 7 225 8 403 9 434

Bowling Analysis	Overs	Mdns.	Runs	Wkts.
P.J. HARTLEY	30	3	128	2
M.A. ROBINSON	29	3	118	2
C.S. PICKLES	14	3	51	0
P. CARRICK	40	10	103	5
J.D. BATTY	8	2	29	0

SUSSEX C.C.C.	SECOND INNINGS	
1.D.M. SMITH		
2.N.J.L. LENHAM		
* 3.P.W.G. PARKER		
4.A.P. WELLS		
5.M.P. SPEIGHT		
6.A.C.S. PIGOTT		
7.A.I.C. DODEMAIDE		
† 8.P. MOORES		
9.I.D.K. SALISBURY		
10.B.T.P. DONELAN		
11.A.N. JONES		
Extras		Total

Fall of Wickets: 1 2 3 4 5 6 7 8 9

Bowling Analysis — Overs Mdns. Runs Wkts.

SUSSEX WON BY AN INNINGS AND 24 RUNS

JOSHUA TETLEY & SON

* Denotes Captain — Umpires: B. DUDDLESTON & A.G.T. WHITEHEAD — Scorers: E.I. LESTER & L.V. CHANDLER — † Denotes Wicket Keeper

Alan Wells – his double hundred beat C.B. Fry's score in 1903 as the highest Sussex score ever against Yorkshire.

Wells remained undefeated on 253, made in 406 minutes from 324 balls and including 3 sixes and 27 fours. It was a momentous innings which beat two records: the highest score made at Acklam Park and the largest individual innings made by a Sussex batsman against Yorkshire, surpassing the 234 made by C.B. Fry at Bradford eighty-eight years before. Sussex were now not to be denied, and the hosts' paltry 171 in their second innings led *Wisden* to note that 'Yorkshire collapsed in some confusion', as Sussex ran out winners by an innings and some runs to spare.

Alan Wells' innings was one of the high points of his 'purple patch' from 1989 to 1995, when he scored almost 10,000 Championship runs at an average in excess of 48, and recorded 29 centuries and 45 fifties. He was then one of the outstanding batsmen in England, but the national selectors managed to include him in only one Test. In the 1992 season, he succeeded Paul Parker and became the County's sixteenth post-war captain, and only one of four to have been born in Sussex. Poor results in 1996 led, sadly, to his dismissal as captain and a move to Kent, where he failed to show much of the great form that had pervaded his time in his native county.

Sussex v. Kent

3, 4, 5 and 6 September 1991 County Championship
Hove

In 1984, Sussex and Kent had tied their match at Hastings, but that low-scoring game was small beer compared with the encounter at Hove seven years later. Kent's first innings was embellished by Neil Taylor's fine 111 and his fourth-wicket partnership of 138 with Matthew Fleming. Sussex, having begun their first innings just before the close on the first day, replied boldly on the second day with the Wells brothers both contributing seventies, although Mark Ealham's tight bowling kept the scoreboard ticking over only slowly.

Kent's adventurous second innings was dominated by the magnificent strokeplay that Taylor again provided. Scoring well over fifty per cent of his side's runs from the bat, he hit 28 fours and a six in just over five-and-a-half hours and, in adding a double hundred to his first-innings century, he equalled his performance against Surrey the previous season.

Kent scored quickly enough to allow Mark Benson to declare and to get Sussex batting again before the close of the third day. They faced the prospect of scoring 437 runs to win the match. Skipper Paul Parker decided to open the innings with Jamie Hall, and their stand of 146 gave Sussex a good start. The middle of the innings was held together by Alan Wells' powerful hundred, which included 20 fours and a six, and was his seventh three-figure score of the season. The County's fourth wicket did not fall until 371, and they were now in sight of a remarkable win. But the West Indian fast bowler, Tony Merrick, had other ideas and, bowling splendidly on a still good batting wicket, took 3 wickets in 10 balls, including both Wells brothers, so that the last 7 wickets went down for 65 runs. The last part of the match was quite dramatic: Sussex, who had scored 400 runs in the fourth innings for the first time since 1939, went into the final over with the scores level and their last pair together. The non-striker, Ian Salisbury, was almost run out off the first ball, and Tony Pigott was caught at slip off the second 'to bring a memorable contest', in the words of *Wisden,* 'to a fitting conclusion.'

The main protagonists on each side, Alan Wells for Sussex and Neil Taylor for Kent, were involved in a remarkably ironic change of Counties in the 1997 season. After Wells had been stripped of the Sussex captaincy in early 1997, just before the momentous AGM which ousted the Committee, he refused to sign a new contract and moved to Kent. Taylor, who had been consigned to oblivion in Kent's Second XI for the 1996 season, saw an opportunity to re-enter first-class cricket and signed for Sussex. Wagers were placed in both Counties about the relative success in terms of averages of the two players – Taylor with 996 runs (average 38.30) seemed to win by a whisker over Wells with 1,055 runs (average 37.67).

Neil Taylor, later a Sussex player – a single century in the first innings and a double in the second.

The Sussex County Cricket Club
Britannic Assurance Championship

RESULT: MATCH TIED
MATCH POINTS: SUSSEX 16 KENT 14

TOSS – KENT ELECTED TO BAT   SUSSEX v KENT

at HOVE   on 3,4,5,6 SEPTEMBER 1991

	SUSSEX	1st Innings		2nd Innings	
1	J W HALL	ct COWDREY b EALHAM	41	bowled MERRICK	52
2	+ P MOORES	bowled MERRICK	8	lbw MERRICK	0
3	K GREENFIELD	ct DAVIS b EALHAM	22	ct COWDREY b MERRICK	0
4	A P WELLS	ct FLEMING b PATEL	74	bowled MERRICK	162
5	*P W G PARKER	ct MARSH b EALHAM	2	lbw b MERRICK	111
6	C M WELLS	bowled MERRICK	76	lbw b MERRICK	34
7	A I C DODEMAIDE	not out	23	ct BENSON b PATEL	25
8	B T P DONELAN	bowled DAVIS	61	run out	2
9	A C S PIGOTT	bowled EALHAM	5	ct COWDREY b PATEL	26
10	I D K SALISBURY	bowled EALHAM	0	not out	1
11	A N JONES	bowled ELLISON	8	bowled MERRICK	1
	b 6 lb 5 wd 6 nb 16	Extras	33	b lb 12 wd 1 nb 9 Extras	22
		(117.5 overs) TOTAL	353	(115.2 overs) TOTAL	436

SCORE AT 100 OVERS 310-6
Bonus Points SUSSEX 4 KENT 2

Runs at fall of wicket	1	2	3	4	5	6	7	8	9	10
1st Innings	8	103	143	147	165	255	331	340	342	
2nd Innings	146	146	254	371	378	378	428	430	434	

Bowling analysis:	O	M	R	W	WB	NB	O	M	R	W	WB	NB
T A MERRICK	24	8	81	2	1	6	27	1	99	7		4
R M ELLISON	22.5	8	68	1	2	1	15	0	59	0	1	1
M V FLEMING	15	3	51	0		5	2	0	9	0		
R P DAVIS	25	5	72	1			32	5	109	0		
M A EALHAM	21	6	39	5	3	4	16	1	80	0		4
M M PATEL	10	2	31	1			23.2	3	68	2		

	KENT	1st Innings		2nd Innings	
1	* M R BENSON	ct MOORES b DODEMAIDE	48	ct MOORES b DODEMAIDE	5
2	T R WARD	ct GREENFIELD b SALISBURY	51	ct DONELAN b DODEMAIDE	38
3	N R TAYLOR	lbw b DODEMAIDE	111	not out	203
4	G R COWDREY	ct GREENFIELD b DODEMAIDE	4	run out	78
5	M A EALHAM	stpd MOORES b DONELAN	26	bowled DODEMAIDE	0
6	M V FLEMING	ct HALL b PIGOTT	69	ct PIGOTT b SALISBURY	20
7	+S A MARSH	ct GREENFIELD b SALISBURY	19	lbw b DODEMAIDE	0
8	R M ELLISON	not out	17	ct MOORES b SALISBURY	1
9	M M PATEL	lbw b PIGOTT	8		
10	R P DAVIS	lbw b SALISBURY	0	not out	29
11	T A MERRICK	ct GREENFIELD b SALISBURY	6		
	b 2 lb 6 wd 1 nb 13	Extras	22	b 4 lb 16 wd 3 nb 11 Extras	34
		(100.4 overs) TOTAL	381	(94 overs) TOTAL	408
				for 7 wkts dec	

SCORE AT 100 OVERS 380-9
Bonus Points KENT 4 SUSSEX 4

Runs at fall of wicket	1	2	3	4	5	6	7	8	9	10
1st Innings	91	123	139	277	309	321	348	349	356	
2nd Innings	30	53	259	288	309	309	310			

Bowling analysis:	O	M	R	W	WB	NB	O	M	R	W	WB	NB
A N JONES	9	0	57	0	1	6	10	1	64	0		4
A I C DODEMAIDE	24	4	64	3		1	22	3	87	4		1
A C S PIGOTT	14.4	0	56	2		1	13	3	44	0		3
C M WELLS	12	3	43	0		1	7	1	30	0		1
B T P DONELAN	14	3	52	1			21	4	61	0		
I D K SALISBURY	27	6	101	4		4	21	3	102	2		2

Hours of Play
1st day 10.30-6.00pm (110)
2nd day 10.30-6.00pm (110)
3rd day 10.30-6.00pm (110)
4th day 10.30-5.30pm (102)

Lunch 12.45-1.25pm
Lunch on 4th day
12.30-1.10pm
Tea Interval 20 mins

UMPIRES:
M J KITCHEN
R A WHITE

SCORERS:
L V CHANDLER
J FOLEY

* Captain † Wicketkeeper

FIRST INNINGS POINTS: awarded only for performances in the first 100 overs.
Batting: 1 point awarded on reaching 150, 200, 250 and 300.
Maximum 4 points.
Bowling: 1 point awarded on reaching 3, 5, 7 and 9 wickets.
Maximum 4 points.
Points for win: 16.
NEW BALL may be claimed on completion of 100 overs.

MATCH HOSTS:

MATCH BALLS:
ROGER & ANNIE HANCOCK

LATEST SCORE

SUSSEX *v.* GLAMORGAN

10 August 1993 NatWest Trophy
Hove

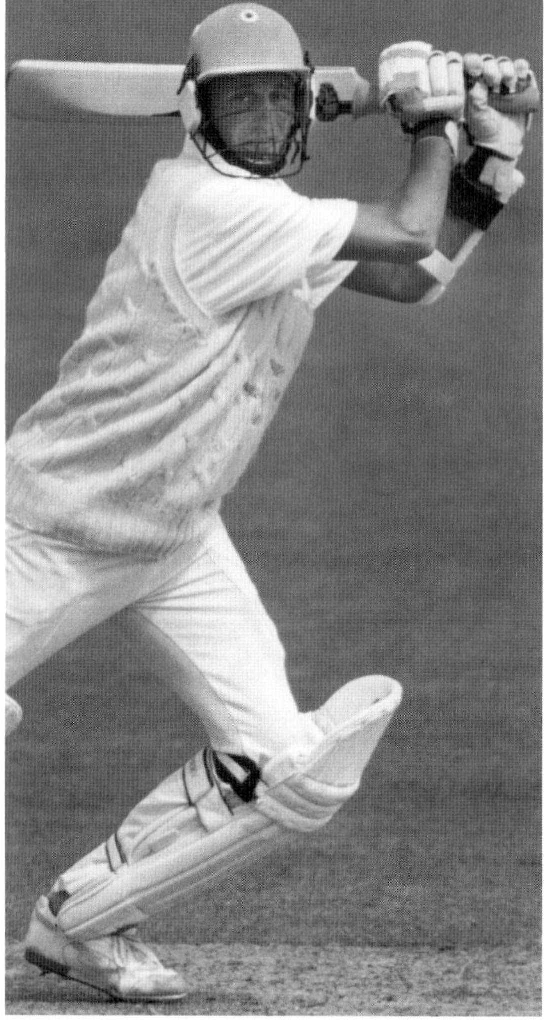

Neil Lenham, with his yellow helmet, helped his skipper turn the game in Sussex's favour.

Both Sussex and Glamorgan had shown good form in the early rounds of the NatWest Trophy in 1993. In the early stages, the Welshmen had Viv Richards' massive 162* to thank for an easy win over Oxfordshire, and a strong Durham side – which included Wayne Larkins, Ian Botham and former Sussex captain, Paul Parker – had been beaten in the second round, when Matthew Maynard's 101 had led them to a 7-wickets victory. The quarter-final saw them overcome Worcestershire by 104 runs and reach the semi-finals of this competition for only the second time. Sussex, likewise, had experienced an easy win in the first round against Wales Minor Counties, and had then disposed of Hampshire, when David Smith and Bill Athey, by adding 248 together, had broken the tournament record for the first wicket. If the quarter-final win over Northamptonshire by 40 runs was less decisive, it was certainly good enough. Franklyn Stephenson and Ed Giddins had bowled well and largely contained Allan Lamb, whose 71 runs were made in only 88 balls. Both Counties, therefore, came to Hove in August expecting to do well.

In front of a crowd of 5,500, which included many Welsh supporters who had made the long trip to Hove, Glamorgan won the toss, but achieved only a fair start with 3 wickets down for 71, while the dismissal of Viv Richards, who was caught and bowled by off-spinner Keith Greenfield, made it 124 for 4 wickets. Matthew Maynard was not so easily cowed and, although Stephenson bowled economically and well towards the end of their innings, Glamorgan were probably reasonably satisfied with 220 in their 60 overs.

The visitors were certainly rather more than satisfied when their attack reduced Sussex to 110 for 6 wickets in the forty-fifth over. The match looked like theirs for the taking, but then Neil Lenham joined skipper Alan Wells. Lenham, normally an opener or top-order batsman in the longer game but down the order in the shorter game, immediately got on to the front foot, and Richards' off-spin disappeared for 25 in 3 overs, while Wells orchestrated the innings masterfully. The Welsh voices in the crowd, so ebullient at one stage, now fell silent as Wells manipulated the wilting Glamorgan attack. On one occasion, off-spinner Robert Croft sought to follow the Sussex captain as he edged away to square leg, only to see him move to the off and the umpire call a wide. When Lenham was bowled at 217, Sussex were nearly there, and with 4 balls left they recorded a remarkable victory, even by their own high standards in this tournament, to reach their eighth Gillette/NatWest final.

The County winning the Trophy will receive a prize of £30,000, the losing Finalists £15,000, the losing Semi-finalists £7,500 each and the losing Quarter-finalists £3,750 each.

30p

TOSS: GLAMORGAN ELECTED TO BAT
RESULT: SUSSEX WON BY 4 WKTS

SUSSEX v GLAMORGAN

MAN OF THE MATCH: A P WELLS

TUESDAY 10TH AUGUST 1993

SUSSEX

	Batsman	How out	Runs	Runs at fall of wicket
1.	D M SMITH	bowled WATKIN	8	1. - 12
2.	C W J ATHEY	ct MAYNARD b DALE	17	2. - 12
3.	M P SPEIGHT	ct LEFEBVRE b WATKIN	0	3. - 42
4.	*A P WELLS	not out	106	4. - 47
5.	K GREENFIELD	run out	1	5. - 86
6.	N J LENHAM	bowled LEFEBVRE	47	6. -110
7.	F D STEPHENSON	ct COTTEY b WATKIN	25	7. -217
8.	+P MOORES	ct RICHARDS b DALE	8	8.
9.	I D K SALISBURY	not out	2	9.
10.	A C S PIGOTT			10.
11.	E S H GIDDINS			11.

B LB 4 WB 4 NB 2 (59.2 overs) Extras 10
TOTAL 224 for 6 wkts

BOWLING ANALYSIS	O	M	R	W	WB	NB
WATKIN	12	2	43	3		
LEFEBVRE	12	4	24	1		
BARWICK	11.2	1	33	0	1	
DALE	12	3	43	2		
CROFT	9	0	52	0	3	
RICHARDS	3	0	25	0		2

GLAMORGAN

	Batsman	How out	Runs	Runs at fall of wicket
1.	S P JAMES	lbw b LENHAM	31	1. - 54
2.	*H MORRIS	bowled PIGOTT	21	2. - 56
3.	A DALE	ct SMITH b PIGOTT	1	3. - 71
4.	M P MAYNARD	ct WELLS b STEPHENSON	84	4. -124
5.	I V A RICHARDS	ct & bowled GREENFIELD	22	5. -138
6.	P A COTTEY	bowled GREENFIELD	1	6. -195
7.	R D B CROFT	bowled SALISBURY	20	7. -204
8.	+C P METSON	ct WELLS b STEPHENSON	8	8. -209
9.	R P LEFEBVRE	not out	8	9. -216
10.	S L WATKIN	bowled STEPHENSON	2	10.
11.	S R BARWICK	bowled PIGOTT	1	11.

B LB 15 WB 6 NB (60 overs) Extras 21
TOTAL 220

BOWLING ANALYSIS	O	M	R	W	WB	NB
STEPHENSON	12	1	25	3	1	
GIDDINS	12	2	46	0		
LENHAM	7	0	31	1	4	
PIGOTT	9	1	23	3	1	
SALISBURY	11	1	45	1		
GREENFIELD	9	1	35	2		

SCORERS: L V CHANDLER B T DENNING
UMPIRES: J C BALDERSTONE K E PALMER

* CAPTAIN + WICKETKEEPER

MATCH ADJUDICATOR: BRIAN LUCKHURST

TOTAL RUNS SCORED AT END OF EACH OVER

OVER	1ST	2ND	OVER	1ST	2ND
1			31		
2			32		
3			33		
4			34		
5			35		
6			36		
7			37		
8			38		
9			39		
10			40		
11			41		
12			42		
13			43		
14			44		
15			45		
16			46		
17			47		
18			48		
19			49		
20			50		
21			51		
22			52		
23			53		
24			54		
25			55		
26			56		
27			57		
28			58		
29			59		
30			60		

SUSSEX *v.* ESSEX

31 August, 1, 2 and 3 September 1993 — County Championship
Hove

Peter Eaton had prepared a belter of a pitch for Sussex's end-of-season match with Essex – a wicket, according to *Wisden,* 'for batsmen to gorge themselves on'. And so it proved. Alan Wells won the toss and took first use of the wicket. Bill Athey went relatively early and, after Neil Lenham's dismissal, Keith Greenfield, whose 107 was his maiden Championship ton, and the skipper put on 183. With Martin Speight weighing in with an unbeaten 75, the County closed on a substantial 392 for 4. The next morning, Speight just failed to reach three figures, but John North went on to become Sussex's third centurion. The Sussex innings closed on 591, their highest total since their 597 for 7 declared against Leicestershire in 1938.

Essex set off after Sussex's total like an express train, and Paul Prichard ran to his hundred off 94 balls and was 123* when Essex closed on 256 for 3. Believe it or not, 847 runs had been made in two days. The third day was not essentially different from the first two, as Prichard went on to complete a double hundred and Graham Gooch decided to declare 98 behind in the hope of forcing a win. When Sussex went in again, openers Neil Lenham and Bill Athey added 228 and, although Athey was dismissed off the penultimate ball of the day and night-watchman Ed Giddins went first ball, the County had extended their lead to 326 and the match total had risen to 1,312. Alan Wells must have pondered overnight how bold a declaration he might make, especially as the wicket was showing no signs of wear. Lenham added a further 28 to his overnight 121, and Greenfield added a fifty to his first-innings ton. With 67 runs added in the first twenty-five minutes, Wells declared, leaving Essex to score 411 in 92 overs. Giddins had Prichard lbw early on, but John Stephenson and Nasser Hussain put on 215 for the second wicket, and then Gooch and Salim Malik joined in an unbroken fourth-wicket stand of 143 to see the visitors home by 7 wickets.

Seven centuries, nine half-centuries and 1,808 runs (at an average of 90.4 runs per wicket) gave this match the highest aggregate of runs for any first-class match played in England, beating the 1,723 in the England *v.* Australia Test of 1948. It was broken only in 2002, when the Surrey/Somerset match produced 7 runs more at an average of over 100 per wicket. The feast of runs was not really quite what Sussex needed: on the following day they scored 321 – the highest innings total in a final – in the NatWest clash at Lord's, only to see it pipped by Warwickshire that very evening, and on the previous Sunday they had made 312 against Hampshire in the Sunday League and lost by 8 wickets. Few sides score 1,536 runs in a week and manage to lose all three games!

Martin Speight just missed his hundred.

John North became Sussex's third centurion.

The Sussex County Cricket Club

RESULT: SUSSEX ELECTED TO BAT ESSEX WON BY 7 WKTS MATCH POINTS: ESSEX 21 SUSSEX 5

Britannic Assurance Championship

SUSSEX v ESSEX

at HOVE on 31 AUGUST, 1,2,3 SEPTEMBER

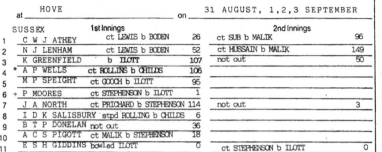

	SUSSEX	1st Innings		2nd Innings	
1	C W J ATHEY	ct LEWIS b BODEN	26	ct SUB b MALIK	96
2	N J LENHAM	ct LEWIS b BODEN	52	ct HUSSAIN b MALIK	149
3	K GREENFIELD	b ILOTT	107	not out	50
4	* A P WELLS	ct ROLLINS b CHILDS	106		
5	M P SPEIGHT	ct GOOCH b ILOTT	95		
6	+ P MOORES	ct STEPHENSON b ILOTT	1		
7	J A NORTH	ct PRICHARD b STEPHENSON	114	not out	3
8	I D K SALISBURY	stpd ROLLING b CHILDS	6		
9	B T P DONELAN	not out	36		
10	A C S PIGOTT	ct MALIK b STEPHENSON	18		
11	E S H GIDDINS	bowled ILOTT	0	ct STEPHENSON b ILOTT	0
12	A EDWARDS				
	b 1 lb 9 wb 6 nb 14	Extras	30	b 6 lb wb 2 nb 6 Extras	14
		TOTAL	591	(69.1 overs) TOTAL for 3 wkts dec	312

SCORE AT 120 OVERS 436-4

Bonus Points SUSSEX 4 ESSEX 1

Runs at fall	1	2	3	4	5	6	7	8	9	10
of wicket (1st)	73	80	263	374	438	444	461	569	591	
(2nd)	228	228	296							

Bowling analysis:	O	M	R	W	WB	NB	O	M	R	W	WB	NB
ILOTT	38.3	11	119	4	4		7.5	0	23	1		
BODEN	25	3	118	2	1	2	10	0	62	0	2	
STEPHENSON	33	8	111	2	1	12	9	1	42	0		6
CHILDS	34	12	104	2			17	4	47	0		
SUCH	26	4	87	0			3	1	11	0		
MALIK	7	0	37	0			18.1	1	88	2		
GOOCH	1	0	5	0								
HUSSAIN							4.1	0	33	0		

	ESSEX	1st Innings		2nd Innings	
1	* G A GOOCH			not out	74
2	J P STEPHENSON	ct WELLS b PIGOTT	9	ct SALISBURY b GREENFIELD	122
3	P J PRICHARD	not out	225	lbw b GIDDINS	24
4	SALIM MALIK	bowled GIDDINS	73	not out	63
5	N HUSSAIN	not out	70	ct ATHEY b GREENFIELD	118
6	J J B LEWIS	ct SALISBURY b LENHAM	43		
7	+ R J ROLLINS				
8	M C ILOTT	bowled SALISBURY	51		
9	D J P BODEN				
10	J H CHILDS				
11	P M SUCH				
12	T D TOPLEY				
	b 4 lb 4 wb 2 nb 12	Extras	22	b 3 lb 3 wb 3 nb 2 Extras	11
	(104.4 overs)	TOTAL for 4 wkts dec	493	(84 overs) TOTAL for 3 wkts	412

Bonus Points ESSEX 4 SUSSEX 1

Runs at fall	1	2	3	4	5	6	7	8	9	10
of wicket (1st)	21	120	254	342						
(2nd)	46	261	269							

Bowling analysis:	O	M	R	W	WB	NB	O	M	R	W	WB	NB
PIGOTT	23	0	127	1		2	12	2	43	0		
GIDDINS	21.4	2	99	1	2	2	10	0	37	1		
NORTH	10	0	52	0			13	0	87	0	3	
DONELAN	14	2	64	0		6	12	1	66	0		
LENHAM	7	1	27	1								
SALISBURY	24	2	94	1		2	23	4	102	0		
ATHEY	5	0	22	0			3	0	31	0		

LATEST SCORE

PHONE RAPID CRICKETLINE
INSTANT SCORES
0891 567515
HOME AND AWAY GAMES

HOURS OF PLAY
1st Day 11-6.30 (110 overs)
2nd Day 11-6.30 (110 overs)
3rd Day 11-6.30 (110 overs)
4th Day 11-6.00 (102 overs)
Lunch 1.15-1.55pm
Lunch on 4th Day 1-1.40pm
Tea Interval 20 minutes

UMPIRES:
J H HARRIS
G I BURGESS

SCORERS:
L V CHANDLER
C F DRIVER

* Captain + Wicketkeeper
FIRST INNINGS POINTS: awarded only for performances in the first 120 overs.

Batting: 1 point awarded on reaching 200, 250, 300 and 350.

Bowling: 1 point awarded on reaching 3,5,7 and 9 wickets. Maximum 4 points.

Points for win: 16
NEW BALL may be claimed on completion of 100 overs.

MATCH HOSTS:
SEEBOARD

MATCH BALLS:
THE PRINCE ALBERT, COPTHORNE

SUSSEX *v.* WARWICKSHIRE

4 September 1993 NatWest Final
Lord's

The thirty-first Gillette/NatWest Lord's final has been recognised as the greatest so far in this series of contests. This thrilling match was a real classic and, for once, the players who shone were not regular stars of the game. For Sussex, it was Martin Speight, the talented painter of cricket grounds, who showed an artistry that delighted the crowd and David Smith, the much-travelled left-hander, who provided the essential backbone of his county's total. Warwickshire matched this duo with Dermot Reeve, once a Sussex man but now his County's captain and something of a one-day specialist, and with Asif Din, the journeyman professional originally from Uganda.

Reeve, on winning the toss, decided to bowl first. Bill Athey fell early, but fireworks erupted when Speight appeared at number three. Sweeping audaciously and jumping down the wicket to the quicker bowlers, he scored a rapid fifty in 51 deliveries. When Alan Wells was deceived by Neil Smith and Franklyn Stephenson went early, Sussex could have faltered at 190 for 4, but Smith and Neil Lenham added a sparkling 119 and the three hundred mark was passed. Warwickshire's fielders were totally demoralised and the final 10 overs produced 81 runs. Off the very last ball of the innings, Smith, the rock on which the Sussex total had been built, was run out. Only later did this attain some significance. In the late afternoon, Sussex must have felt that a fifth title was close to being theirs and, as the day wore on, the early editions of the Sunday papers were talking of a notable Sussex success!

Warwickshire's task looked daunting, even more so when both openers were dismissed with only 18 on the board. Ostler and Paul Smith, aptly described by *Wisden* as 'all long hair and long handle', added 75, but when the former went at 93, Asif Din came to the wicket. 'Gunga' had been a professional at Edgbaston for twelve years and only rarely had made his mark, but this day was to belong to him. Smith, driving powerfully, and Asif, all wristy cuts and sweeps, added a further 71 and Sussex's out-cricket was beginning to look as ragged as their opponents' had done earlier. When Smith went at 164 for 4, Asif and Reeve needed to score 158 in 24 overs, better than a run per ball. With the total on 306, Asif, who had added 142 with Reeve, was caught at deep cover. Just two overs were left, 20 more runs were still needed and Giddins, bowling the fifty-ninth over, conceded a niggardly 5 runs, so that 15 were required from Stephenson's final over in the now prevailing twilight. Reeve managed 13 from the first 5 balls and, when Twose, facing his only ball of the match, pushed it for 2, Warwickshire were home with the highest total recorded in a 60-over final.

A truism perhaps, but neither side deserved to lose this match. Warwickshire had sneaked home worthily, and even the most fervent Sussex supporter recognised that.

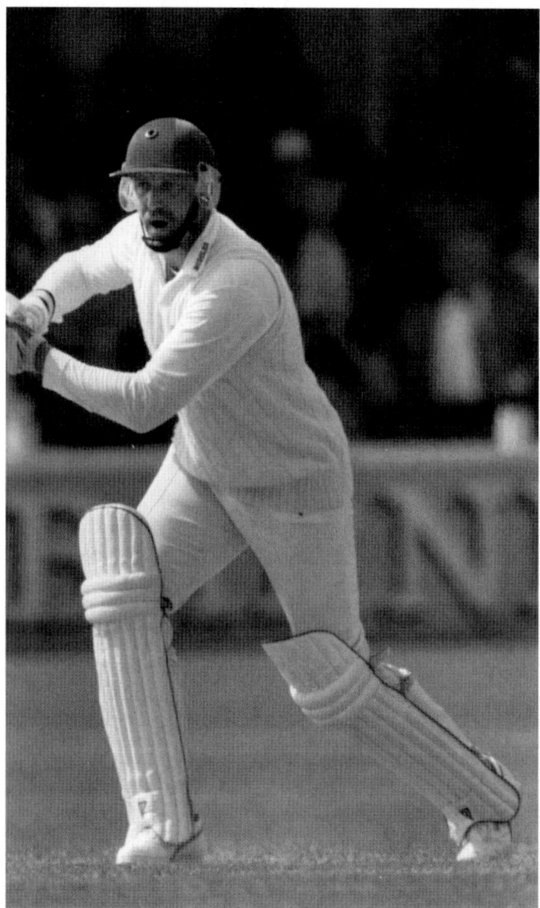

David Smith batted through the Sussex innings.

MAJOR MATCHES AT LORD'S – 1994

ENGLAND v NEW ZEALAND
(Texaco Trophy)
Saturday, 21st May

ENGLAND v NEW ZEALAND
(Cornhill Test Match)
Thursday, 16th to Monday 20th, June

ENGLAND v SOUTH AFRICA
(Cornhill Test Match)
Thursday, 21st to Monday 25th, July

Application forms for the above matches may be obtained from the Club Office after 1st January, 1994, and tickets will be allocated to the general public by ballot on 1st March, 1994.

The demand for tickets in 1994 is expected to be very high; therefore, all applicants are advised to return their completed forms by 28th February, 1994.

An application form may be reserved at any time by writing to M.C.C. Tickets, Lord's Ground, London, NW8 8QN.
All enquiries will be acknowledged but no forms will be sent before the end of this year.

BENSON and HEDGES CUP – FINAL
Saturday, 9th July

NATWEST BANK TROPHY – FINAL
Saturday, 3rd September

Public stand tickets for the one-day finals are offered to the First-Class County Cricket Clubs for sale to their members. However, any tickets which remain unallocated by this method are offered for sale by M.C.C. to the general public from the following dates:

Benson and Hedges Cup – Final — Tuesday, 31st May
NatWest Bank Trophy – Final — Monday, 1st August

There is no application form for these matches. Any available tickets will be sold to personal callers at the Ground or to those who telephone the Club's credit card telephone line (071-289 5005) and wish to pay for their tickets by that method. Access and Visa credit card bookings are accepted on the above telephone number between the hours of 10.00a.m. and 4.00p.m., Mondays to Fridays.

WARNING

Genuine tickets for matches at Lord's are obtainable only from M.C.C. or its authorised agents. Any person selling tickets for an amount of money above the value printed on the tickets is doing so without the Club's permission. Some tickets offered for sale in this manner are stolen and the purchasers or holders of such tickets will be interviewed by the Metropolitan Police before being removed from the Ground.

MARYLEBONE CRICKET CLUB

NatWest Bank Trophy Final

SUSSEX v. WARWICKSHIRE

at Lord's Ground, †Saturday, September 4th, 1993

SUSSEX

	Batsman	How out	Runs
1	D. M. Smith	run out	124
2	C. W. J. Athey	c Piper b Munton	0
3	M. P. Speight	c Piper b Reeve	50
‡4	A. P. Wells	b N. Smith	33
5	F. D. Stephenson	c N. Smith b Twose	3
6	N. J. Lenham	l b w b Reeve	58
7	K. Greenfield	not out	8
*8	P. Moores		
9	I. D. K. Salisbury		
10	A. C. S. Pigott		
11	E. S. H. Giddins		
	B , l-b 11, w 18, n-b 16,		45
		Total...	321

FALL OF THE WICKETS

1...4 2...107 3...183 4...190 5...309 6...321 7... 8... 9... 10...

Bowling Analysis	O.	M.	R.	W.	Wd.	N-b
Small	12	0	71	0	7	...
Munton	9	0	67	1	6	4
P. Smith	7	0	45	0	1	6
Reeve	12	1	60	2	1	6
N. Smith	12	1	37	1	1	...
Twose	8	1	30	1	2	...

WARWICKSHIRE

	Batsman	How out	Runs
1	A. J. Moles	c Moores b Pigott	2
2	J. D. Ratcliffe	b Stephenson	13
3	D. P. Ostler	c Smith b Salisbury	25
4	P. A. Smith	c Moores b Stephenson	60
5	Asif Din	c Speight b Giddins	104
‡6	D. A. Reeve	not out	81
7	R. G. Twose	not out	2
8	N. M. K. Smith		
*9	K. J. Piper		
10	G. C. Small		
11	T. A. Munton		
	B 3, l-b 13, w 13, n-b 6,		35
		Total...	322

FALL OF THE WICKETS

1...18 2...18 3...93 4...164 5...306 6... 7... 8... 9... 10...

Bowling Analysis	O.	M.	R.	W.	Wd.	N-b
Giddins	12	0	57	1	4	...
Stephenson	12	2	51	2	1	2
Pigott	11	0	74	1	5	4
Salisbury	11	0	59	1	1	...
Greenfield	7	0	31	0	2	...
Lenham	7	0	34	0	...	...

Any alterations to teams will be announced over the public address system

‡ Captain * Wicket-keeper

Umpires—H. D. Bird & M. J. Kitchen Scorers—L. V. Chandler, A. E. Davis & E. Solomon

Luncheon Interval 12.45 p.m.—1.25 p.m. Tea Interval will be 20 minutes and will normally be taken at 4.30 p.m.

†This match is intended to be completed in one day, but three days have been allocated in case of weather interference.

Warwickshire won the toss and elected to field

Warwickshire won by 5 wickets

Total runs scored at end of each over:

First Innings

1	2	3	4	5	6	7	8	9	10	11	12	13	14	15	16	17	18	19	20
21	22	23	24	25	26	27	28	29	30	31	32	33	34	35	36	37	38	39	40
41	42	43	44	45	46	47	48	49	50	51	52	53	54	55	56	57	58	59	60

Second Innings

1	2	3	4	5	6	7	8	9	10	11	12	13	14	15	16	17	18	19	20
21	22	23	24	25	26	27	28	29	30	31	32	33	34	35	36	37	38	39	40
41	42	43	44	45	46	47	48	49	50	51	52	53	54	55	56	57	58	59	60

SUSSEX *v.* DURHAM

6, 7, 8 and 10 June 1996 — County Championship
Hove

Ian Salisbury – a spell of 5 wickets for 0 runs.

Keith Greenfield won his county cap in his tenth season.

Durham did not become a first-class County until 1992 and, almost inevitably, the club struggled somewhat in their early years in the Championship. The match between the two sides in 1996 led to Sussex's fifth successive win against the fledgling County and, for the second season running, the Sussex innings contained three batsmen reaching their hundreds.

Peter Eaton, Sussex's groundsman, had produced a splendid pitch and Alan Wells, on winning the toss, had no hesitation in batting on a scorcher of a morning. Although the left-arm over-the-wicket pace of Simon Brown soon knocked back the off-stump of County debutant, Toby Radford, Bill Athey and Alan Wells settled down to a productive second-wicket partnership of 196, and the County ended the first day happily placed at 302 for 4 wickets. Durham were Athey's rabbits and he scored his fourth successive ton against them (having missed the first encounter) and Wells, still in the middle of the purple patch which characterised his batting in the 1990s, stroked an effortless 113 before being brilliantly caught at slip by West Indian Test player, Sherwin Campbell. Keith Greenfield, who was shown in the morning papers as having been dismissed for 38, was, in fact, 37* and the following day, as Sussex moved to a massive 552 for 8 declared, he scored a Championship-best hundred, a patient 124* in a stay of over six hours. For his pains, in his tenth season as a county cricketer, he was awarded his County cap.

After Sussex declared, Durham were put to the sword by Ian Salisbury. Not always known for his accuracy – the fate perhaps of many wrist-spinners – on this occasion he was wholly on song and, in a spell of 15 balls, took 5 wickets for no runs as Durham collapsed from 99 for 1 wicket to 159 all out. Thoroughly demoralised, they were invited to follow-on some 393 runs adrift. Danny Law, brought on early in the Durham second innings, emulated Salisbury and ripped out the first 5 opposition wickets (like Salisbury, for no runs) although he required 25 balls to do so. At this point, the visitors, in the shape of Campbell and 'keeper Chris Scott (perhaps better known for having dropped Brian Lara on 20, when the latter went on to make 501), staged a recovery. Campbell and Scott added 129 for the sixth wicket and finally Melvyn Betts and David Cox denied Sussex a three-day triumph. They took the score from 223 for 9 to 324 without further loss by the close of play. Sadly for them, however, they added only 2 further runs in 7 balls on the final morning before Cox was dismissed and Sussex were home by a massive margin.

SUSSEX COUNTY CRICKET CLUB
Britannic Assurance Championship

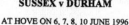

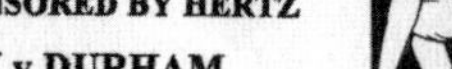
MATCH SPONSORED BY HERTZ

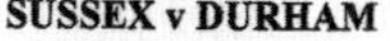
SUSSEX v DURHAM

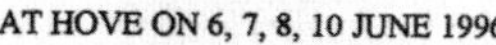
AT HOVE ON 6, 7, 8, 10 JUNE 1996

TOSS - SUSSEX ELECTED TO BAT

RESULT - SUSSEX WON BY AN INNINGS & 67 RUNS

MATCH POINTS: SUSSEX 24 DURHAM 1

SUSSEX

	1st Innings		2nd Innings	
1	T A RADFORD bowled BROWN	1		
2	C W J ATHEY lbw b BIRBECK	102		
3	* A P WELLS ct CAMPBELL b BIRBECK	113		
4	K GREENFIELD not out	124		
5	N J LENHAM lbw b BROWN	10		
6	D R C LAW run out	35		
7	+ P MOORES ct BOILING b BIRBECK	4		
8	I D K SALISBURY ct BETTS b COX	22		
9	V C DRAKES ct SCOTT b COX	56		
10	J D LEWRY not out	28		
11	E S H GIDDINS			
	b 1 lb 15 wb 3 nb 38 Extras	57	b lb wb nb Extras	
	(163.5 overs) Total	552	Total	
	for 8 wkts			

Bonus Points Sussex 4 Durham 1
Score at 120 overs 368-4

Runs at fall	1 - 15	2 - 211	3 - 288	4 - 302	5 - 369	6 - 373	7 - 411	8 - 515	9	10
of wicket	1	2	3	4	5	6	7	8	9	10

Bowling Analysis	o	m	r	w	wb	nb	o	m	r	w	wb	nb
BROWN	35	10	96	2	1	1						
BETTS	22	1	148	0	2	14						
BIRBECK	31	9	88	3		2						
BOILIING	34	10	74	0								
COX	40	10	116	2								
BLENKIRON	1.5	0	14	0								

HOURS OF PLAY:
1st Day 11-6.30pm (104 overs)
2nd Day 11-6.30pm (104 overs)
3rd Day 11-6.30pm (104 overs)
4th Day 11-6.00pm (96 overs)
Lunch 1.15-1.55pm
Lunch on 4th Day 1-1.40pm
Tea Interval 20 minutes

* Captain + Wicketkeeper

FIRST INNINGS POINTS:
awarded only for performances in the first 120 overs.

Batting: 1 point awarded on reaching 200, 250, 300 and 350.
Maximum 4 points.

Bowling: 1 point awarded on reaching 3, 5, 7 and 9 wickets.
Maximum 4 points.

Points for a draw: 3 each side.

Points for a win: 16.

DURHAM

	1st Innings		2nd Innings	
1	S L CAMPBELL ct GREENFIELD b GIDDINS	45	lbw b DRAKES	87
2	* M A ROSEBERRY bowled GIDDINS	34	ct & bowled LAW	11
3	J E MORRIS ct WELLS b SALISBURY	12	lbw b LAW	0
4	D A BLENKIRON stpd MOORES b SALISBURY	22	lbw b LAW	3
5	P D COLLINGWOOD ct MOORES b SALISBURY	16	ct MOORES b LAW	5
6	S D BIRBECK lbw b SALISBURY	0	ct & bowled LAW	8
7	+ C W SCOTT ct MOORES b SALISBURY	0	ct WELLS b DRAKES	52
8	M M BETTS ct DRAKES b SALISBURY	0	not out	57
9	S J E BROWN ct GREENFIELD b DRAKES	12	ct MOORES b SALISBURY	16
10	J BOILING ct SALISBURY b DRAKES	4	bowled SALISBURY	1
11	D M COX not out	4	bowled GIDDINS	67
	b 2 lb 2 wb nb 6 Extras	10	b 1 lb 6 wb 1 nb 11 Extras	19
	(44.1 overs) Total	159	(78.1 overs) Total	326

Bonus Points Durham 0 Sussex 4

Runs at fall	1 - 71	2 - 99	3 - 119	4 - 132	5 - 132	6 - 136	7 - 136	8 - 139	9 - 152	10 - 159
of wicket	1 - 24	2 - 24	3 - 28	4 - 40	5 - 50	6 - 129	7 - 180	8 - 185	9 - 223	10

Bowling Analysis	o	m	r	w	wb	nb	o	m	r	w	wb	nb
DRAKES	11.1	3	46	2			15	2	84	2		3
LEWRY	8	3	28	0			10	0	57	0	1	
LAW	4	0	30	0			12	4	33	5		1
SALISBURY	11	6	15	6			26	5	84	2		
GIDDINS	10	1	36	2		3	12.1	2	56	1		1
GREENFIELD							3	2	5	0		

NEW BALL may be claimed on completion of 100 overs.

UMPIRES:

T E JESTY
M J KITCHEN

SCORERS:

L V CHANDLER
B HUNT

MATCH BALLS:

PRINCE ALBERT
PUBLIC HOUSE,
COPTHORNE

Sussex *v.* Derbyshire

29 July 1997
Derby

NatWest Trophy

'Thank God they did not sign him', referring to the fact that Surrey had at one time been interested in Rajesh Rao, is how Tony Pigott, then the County's Chief Executive, expressed his delight when the Ugandan-born batsman produced one of the outstanding one-day innings of recent times, as he led Sussex to victory in the quarter-final of the NatWest Trophy at Derby in 1997. He might conceivably have added: 'Thank God *I* didn't sign him', as Pigott was Surrey's Second XI coach at the time when Rao was playing for Surrey Colts!

Sussex had done well in the 1997 NatWest Trophy, beating Shropshire in first round, and in the second they had romped past Lancashire's 283 for 6 with 3.5 overs left, as Keith Greenfield with a hundred and Mark Newell with an unbeaten 75 took the honours. Rao was not selected as a first choice for the quarter-final against Derbyshire. On the morning of the match, however, Neil Lenham pulled out injured and the twenty-two-year-old's chance had come. The hosts took first knock, and their innings was built round a magnificent unbeaten hundred from Chris Adams, who was to become, ironically enough, Sussex's captain in the following season. This was his fifth one-day ton of the season, and the home side had every reason to feel that they had done enough. Sussex needed nearly 5.5 runs an over against an attack which contained three Test match bowlers. It seemed a tall order.

Sussex's challenge became even more severe when Greenfield, the hero of the win against Lancashire, was clean bowled by the third ball of Devon Malcolm's opening over. Rao was quite undaunted and, with a series of powerful leg-side boundaries, hit the former England bowler out of the attack. DeFreitas and Cork did no better against him and, although Bill Athey and Mark Newell made only modest contributions, Rao joined in a fourth-wicket partnership of 110 with Neil Taylor, before he was dismissed. His 158 had been made off 165 balls and contained 18 fours. Although Taylor went soon afterwards, the momentum was there, and Keith Newell and skipper Peter Moores had little difficulty in reaching the required total. It was an extraordinary achievement, as it was the highest score made by a team chasing a total in the competition, surpassing even Warwickshire's 322 when they beat Sussex in the 1993 final at Lord's. Sadly, however, it was not the start of a glorious career for Rajesh Rao. His subsequent form was patchy, both at first-class and one-day level, and he was not retained for the 2000 season.

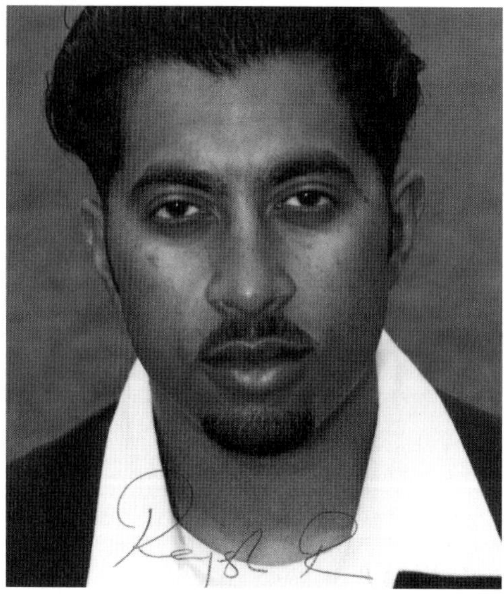

Rajesh Rao – played in the match owing to Lenham's injury.

Neil Taylor.

Derbyshire won the toss and elected to bat

DERBYSHIRE

A.S. Rollins	lbw b Drakes	40	
D.G. Cork	b Drakes	16	
C.J. Adams	not out	129	
#K.M. Krikken	st Moores b Khan	38	
K.J. Barnett	c and b Robinson	18	
G.A. Khan	b Robinson	0	
V.P. Clarke	c Taylor b Robinson	11	
*P.A.J. DeFreitas	c Rao b Drakes 26		
P. Aldred	c Moores b Drakes	4	
A.J. Harris	not out	5	
D.E. Malcolm	did not bat		
Extras	(lb21, w9, nb10)	40	1/38, 2/74, 3/138, 4/201, 5/203
TOTAL	(8 wkts, 60 overs)	327	6/249, 7/298, 8/316

Bowling	O	M	R	W
Drakes	12	0	62	4
Jarvis	9	0	53	0
Khan	12	1	48	1
Robinson	11	0	59	3
K. Newell	4	0	17	0
Greenfield	12	0	67	0

SUSSEX

K. Greenfield	b Malcolm	0	
C.W.J. Athey	b Clarke	30	
R.K. Rao	c Khan b Harris	158	
M. Newell	run out	32	
N.R. Taylor	c Barnett b Cook	48	
K. Newell	not out	29	
*#P. Moores	not out	19	
V.C. Drakes, P.W. Jarvis, A.A. Khan and M.A. Robinson did not bat			
Extras	(lb5, w2, nb 6)	13	1/0, 2/101, 3/168, 4/278, 5/289
TOTAL	(5 wkts, 59.2 overs)	329	

Bowling	O	M	R	W
Malcolm	6	0	33	1
DeFreitas	8	1	43	0
Aldred	6	0	35	0
Cork	11.2	0	67	1
Clarke	11	0	42	1
Barnett	7	0	37	0
Harris	10	0	67	1

Umpires: H.D. Bird and G. Sharp

Sussex won by 5 wickets

SUSSEX *v.* GLOUCESTERSHIRE

19, 20, 21 and 22 May 1999 County Championship
Hove

In defeating Gloucestershire in the course of the 139th over of the second innings, Sussex achieved perhaps the most remarkable victory in the club's history. By scoring 455 for 8 wickets, they had reached their own highest fourth-innings total, the eighth highest ever to win a first-class match and the second highest in a Championship win, the last bettered only by Middlesex's 502 for 6 wickets which defeated Nottinghamshire in 1925. Mark Alleyne won the toss for the visitors, and an opening stand of 113 between Jack Russell and Tim Hancock set them on course for a sound total. Russell's batting has always been idiosyncratic, and his 64 took some five-and-a-half hours, but at 256 for 8 at the close of the first day, the visitors must have been reasonably content.

The next day proved even better for Gloucestershire. At the close, with 9 second-innings wickets in hand, they were 203 runs ahead of Sussex. For a county that had suffered three defeats in their first four Championship matches, they had done well. They had bowled their hosts out for 145 – David Gilbert, Sussex's Chief Executive, reckoned that his side should have made at least 350 – and they had managed to avoid the follow-on only as a result of a last-wicket partnership of 31 between James Kirtley and Mark Robinson. The visitors consolidated their grip on the match in the course of the third day. Russell was again wholly adhesive and took nearly five hours over his 85, which meant that, in addition to keeping wicket, he had spent ten-and-a-half hours batting – certainly no mean achievement in terms of concentration. Windows' half-century was well made and Harvey's straight six off Kirtley was probably the shot of the day. After the visitors' declaration, Sussex needed 452 to win and, with Montgomerie being trapped lbw by Harvey, Adams caught at gully and Peirce at point, they ended the day on 127 for 3 wickets. The Gloucester team at this point must have fancied an early return to the West Country.

The next day was, however, to alter everything. Michael Di Venuto, the Tasmanian batsman so cleverly recruited by David Gilbert to fill the place left vacant by Michael Bevan, was 56* overnight and he and Welshman Tony Cottey now joined in a fourth-wicket partnership of 256 in 73 overs before Di Venuto, who had faced 257 balls and hit 22 fours, was lbw to the Gloucester skipper. Both batsmen had made their maiden hundreds for their adopted County and Cottey, whose innings lasted 275 balls and contained 13 fours, marshalled the tail with such skill that victory gradually became a possibility. Umer Rashid, batting with fluency and making what then was his highest score for the County, clinched an incredible win against all odds with 3 balls left. Cricket rarely gets better than this.

Umar Rashid's drive brings Sussex close to victory.

SUSSEX C.C.C

PPP HEALTHCARE COUNTY CHAMPIONSHIP

SUSSEX v GLOUCESTERSHIRE

AT HOVE ON 19,20,21,22 MAY 1999

SUSSEX

	1st Innings		2nd Innings	
1	R R MONTGOMERIE lbw b SMITH	12	lbw b HARVEY	6
2	M T E PEIRCE ct SNAPE b LEWIS	14	ct BARNETT b SNAPE	26
3	*C J ADAMS b HARVEY	9	(4) ct SNAPE b HARVEY	15
4	M J DI VENUTO b HARVEY	10	(3) lbw ALLEYNE	162
5	P A COTTEY c RUSSELL b SMITH	20	(5) c RUSSELL b LEWIS	126
6	R K RAO c SNAPE b HARVEY	1	(6) lbw b SMITH	13
7	R S C MARTIN-JENKINS lbw b SMITH	22	(7) c RUSSELL b LEWIS	15
8	U B A RASHID c ALLEYNE b GANNON	13	(8) not out	44
9	+S HUMPHRIES c RUSSELL b SMITH	7	(9) lbw HARVEY	12
10	R K KIRTLEY not out	11	(10) not out	5
11	M A ROBINSON b LEWIS	10		
12	A D EDWARDS			
	b-8 lb-6 wb-2 nb-0	Extras 16	b-13 lb-4 wb-0 nb-14	Extras 31
	(55.5 overs)	Total 145	(138.3 overs)	Total 455/8

Bonus Points

Runs at fall of wicket										
1st Innings	1-26	2-26	3-45	4-50	5-60	6-79	7-104	8-110	9-114	10-145
2nd Innings	1-23	2-46	3-72	4-328	5-360	6-381	7-398	8-429	9	10

Bowling Analysis	o	m	r	w	wb	nb	o	m	r	w	wb	nb
A.M. SMITH	15.0	4	36	4	0	0	23.3	5	60	1	0	3
J. LEWIS	17.5	6	34	2	0	0	15.0	1	70	2	0	1
I.J. HARVEY	13.0	5	24	3	0	0	30.0	4	109	3	0	1
B.W. GANNON	10.0	2	37	1	1	0	8.0	0	33	0	0	2
M.C.J BALL							29.0	5	67	0	0	0
J.N. SNAPE							19.0	5	54	1	0	0
M.W. ALLEYNE							14.0	2	45	1	0	0

GLOUCESTERSHIRE

	1st Innings		2nd Innings	
1	K J BARNETT b MARTIN-JENKINS	4	(3) c HUMPHRIES b ROBINSON	3
2	T H C HANCOCK b MARTIN-JENKINS	66	(1) b MARTIN-JENKINS	29
3	I HARVEY stpd HUMPHRIES b ADAMS	27	(6) c RASHID b KIRTLEY	26
4	M G N WINDOWS lbw b ROBINSON	0	(4) c MONTGOMERIE b KIRTLEY	50
5	*M W ALLEYNE ct & b RASHID	12	(5) c DI VENUTO b ROBINSON	48
6	J N SNAPE ct MARTIN-JENKINS b ADAMS	15	(7) lbw ROBINSON	0
7	+R C RUSSELL b ADAMS	64	(2) c HUMPHRIES b ROBINSON	85
8	M C J BALL not out	43	(8) not out	25
9	J LEWIS ct MARTIN-JENKINS b RASHID	27	(9) c HUMPHRIES b KIRTLEY	12
10	A M SMITH lbw MARTIN-JENKINS	6	(10) not out	7.
11	B W GANNON ct MONTGOMERIE b ROBINSON	9		
12	R I DAWSON			
	b 5 lb 6 wb 4 nb 6	Extras 21	b-11 lb-4 wb-0 nb-2	Extras 17
	(115.2 overs)	Total 294		Total 302 (8wkts dec)

Bonus Points

Runs at fall of wicket										
1st Innings	1-113	2-117	3-120	4-150	5-183	6-206	7-207	8-250	9-262	10-294
2nd Innings	1-42	2-54	3-126	4-211	5-254	6-254	7-254	8-270	9	10

Bowling Analysis	o	m	r	w	wb	nb	o	m	r	w	wb	nb
KIRTLEY	31.0	10	77	0	2	2	20	4	75	4	0	0
MARTIN-JENKINS	24.0	4	85	3	0	0	20.0	6	66	1	0	0
ROBINSON	24.2	6	45	2	0	1	22.0	7	79	3	0	1
ADAMS	14.0	2	37	3	0	0	11	3	31	0	0	0
RASHID	21.0	10	38	2	0	0	12	4	36	0	0	0
RAO	1.0	0	1	0	0	0						

SUSSEX WON BY 2 WICKETS: SUSSEX 16 PTS GLOUCS 6 PTS

HOURS OF PLAY:
1st Day 11-6.30pm (104 overs)
2nd Day 11-6.30pm (104 overs)
3rd Day 11-6.30pm (104 overs)
4th Day 11-6.00pm (96 overs)
Lunch 1st, 2nd, 3rd Days: 1.15pm-1.55pm
4th Day:- 1.00-1.40pm

Tea Interval 1st, 2nd, 3rd Days: 4.10-4.30pm or when 32 overs remain to be bowled, whichever is the later. 4th Day: 3.40-4.00pm

* Captain + Wicketkeeper

FIRST INNINGS POINTS: awarded only for performances in the first 120 overs.
Batting: 1 point awarded on reaching 200, 250, 300 and 350.
Maximum 4 points.
Bowling: 1 point awarded on reaching 3, 5, 7 and 9 wickets.
Maximum 4 points.
Points for a draw: 4 each side.
Points for a win: 12
.NEW BALL may be claimed on completion of 100 overs

UMPIRES:
T E JESTY
B LEADBEATER

SCORERS:
L V CHANDLER
K T GERRISH

MAIN SPONSOR:
THE BAULCH GROUP
FLOODLIGHTS:
STONEGATE FARMERS
OFFICIAL PARTNERS:
IDENTILAM
SAMMONS GROUP
COURAGE BREWERY
OFFICIAL SUPPLIERS:
SETYRES
R T WILLIAMS
POSTURITE
GROUND SPONSOR:
BGP GROUP

GLOS WON THE TOSS & ELECTED TO BAT

SUSSEX *v.* HAMPSHIRE

6 and 7 July 2001 County Championship
Hove

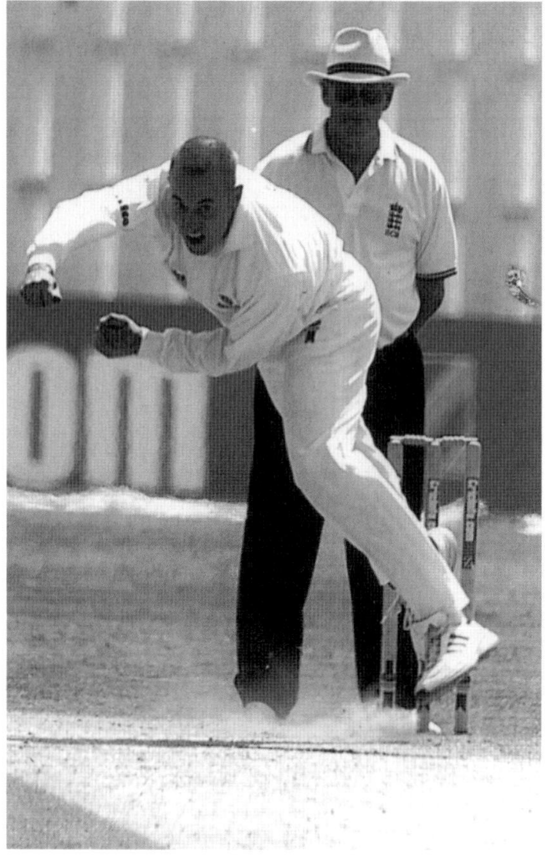

Jason Lewry – a hat-trick and 7 wickets in 13 balls.

Sussex have not always had it their own way with their close neighbours, but the Hampshire expedition to Hove on this occasion proved disastrous for them. The cynic on the Sussex side might have added that it gave the County's players two extra days' holiday.

There was low cloud and a mugginess in the air on the Friday morning when Chris Adams won the toss and immediately inserted Hampshire. The conditions were tailor-made for Jason Lewry to exploit his swing and pace, and he soon had the visitors' openers back in the pavilion. When Billy Taylor, who was playing only because Mark Robinson had injured his back, was introduced into attack, he made an immediate impact. In the space of 3 balls, he ripped the middle out of Hampshire's batting, trapping skipper Robin Smith leg before and having overseas signing Neil Johnson caught by Adams at slip. Although Will Kendall resisted gamely throughout much of the innings, Lewry came back to finish off the tail in no time at all, the last 5 wickets going down for 5 runs. Kendall and Alan Mullally were last out, both lbw to successive balls. The conditions were no more favourable to Sussex, but they showed far greater application than their opponents had done and, although Richard Montgomerie and Murray Goodwin went early, Chris Adams was in sparkling form, hitting Mascarenhas for 3 fours in 1 over and striking Shaun Udal for a straight six. When the close came, Sussex were on 220 for 7 wickets, a lead of 139.

The Saturday proved no less successful for the County. Michael Yardy (34* overnight) soon lost James Kirtley and Lewry, but a last-wicket stand with Taylor produced 66 runs, which gave Sussex a commanding lead of 221. The Lewry show then began all over again. With the third, fourth and fifth balls of his opening over, he produced a hat-trick – the second of his career – to have Kenway caught at short-leg, and Kendall and Smith both lbw. In the course of thirteen balls, spanning the two Hampshire innings, he had taken 7 wickets. This feat, ironically against Sussex, has been bettered only by Pat Pocock of Surrey, who took 7 wickets in 11 balls at the Saffrons in 1972. In the meantime, Johnson and Mascarenhas had steadied the Hampshire ship, but then Lewry returned to have Mascarenhas caught in the gully in his seventh over. In the next, he picked off three more batsmen: off the second ball, Johnson was caught behind and off the fourth and fifth, Adrian Aymes and Alex Morris both perished. Was a double hat-trick on the cards? Unfortunately, it wasn't: the last ball of the over went harmlessly down the leg side and Lewry's remarkable performance (13 for 79 in the match) was dented a little by Udal's long handle, before Kirtley and Taylor wrapped up the resistance as rain began to come in from the sea end.

SUSSEX C.C.C

SUSSEX v HAMPSHIRE

at Hove on 6th, 7th, 8th & 9th July 2001

Cricinfo County Championship Division 2

* = Captain + = Wicketkeeper Sussex Won Toss And Elected To Field

Sussex

	1st Innings				2nd Innings		
1	R.R. MONTGOMERIE		b A. MORRIS	7			
2	M.W. GOODWIN	LBW	b A. MORRIS	9			
3	C.J. ADAMS*		b MULLALLY	71			
4	B. ZUIDERENT	c KENWAY	b TREMLETT	20			
5	M.H. YARDY	NOT OUT		87			
6	U.B.A RASHID	c KENDALL	b MULLALLY	15			
7	M.J. PRIOR+	LBW	b JOHNSON	15			
8	M.J.G. DAVIS	c AYMES	b MASCARENHAS	19			
9	R.J. KIRTLEY	c AYMES	b MULLALLY	4			
10	J.D. LEWRY	c MASCARENHAS	b A. MORRIS	6			
11	B.V. TAYLOR	c JOHNSON	b MASCARENHAS	11			
12	W.J. HOUSE						

b 4	lb 12	wd 6	nb 16	Field Pens 0	Extras	38	b	lb	wd	nb	Extras	
	Pens In Other Inns: 0				Provisional Total	302	Pens In Other Inns				Provisional Total	
	Overs	82.3	Wkts	10	Total	302	Overs		Wkts		Total	

Fall of wickets											
1st Inns:	1st - 14	2nd - 19	3rd - 51	4th - 129	5th - 151	6th - 172	7th - 213	8th - 221	9th - 236	10th - 302
2nd Inns:	1st -	2nd -	3rd -	4th -	5th -	6th -	7th -	8th -	9th -	10th -

BONUS POINTS: SUSSEX 3, HAMPSHIRE 3 New Ball on completion of 100 overs.

Bowling Analysis	Ovs	Md	R	Wk	wd	nb	Ovs	Md	R	Wk	wd	nb
MULLALLY	20.0	4	75	3	0	3						
A. MORRIS	19.0	2	68	3	0	4						
MASCARENHAS	11.3	3	38	2	0	1						
TREMLETT	7.0	1	28	1	2	0						
UDAL	10.0	1	28	0	0	0						
JOHNSON	15.0	0	49	1	1	0						

Hampshire

	1st Innings				2nd Innings		
1	G.W. WHITE	c PRIOR	b LEWRY	9		b KIRTLEY	5
2	D.A. KENWAY	LBW	b LEWRY	18	c MONTGOMERIE	b LEWRY	0
3	W.S. KENDALL	LBW	b LEWRY	22	LBW	b LEWRY	0
4	R.A. SMITH*	LBW	b TAYLOR	7	LBW	b LEWRY	0
5	N.C. JOHNSON	c ADAMS	b TAYLOR	0	c PRIOR	b LEWRY	19
6	C.T. TREMLETT	NOT OUT		2	c ADAMS	b KIRTLEY	10
7	A.D. MASCARENHAS	c YARDY	b ADAMS	8	c GOODWIN	b LEWRY	7
8	A.N. AYMES+		b LEWRY	6	LBW	b LEWRY	8
9	S.D. UDAL	c MONTGOMERIE	b LEWRY	2	NOT OUT		40
10	A.C. MORRIS	LBW	b KIRTLEY	0		b LEWRY	0
11	A.D. MULLALLY	LBW	b LEWRY	0	c KIRTLEY	b TAYLOR	17
12	L.R. PRITTIPAUL						

b 0	lb 1	wd 2	nb 4	Field Pens 0	Extras	7	b 0	lb 2	wd 0	nb 0	Extras	2
	Pens In Other Inns: 0				Provisional Total	81	Pens In Other Inns				Provisional Total	108
	Overs	44.4	Wkts	10	Total	81	Overs	24.2	Wkts	10	Total	108

Fall of wickets										
1st Inns:	1st - 28	2nd - 29	3rd - 42	4th - 42	5th - 68	6th - 76	7th - 78	8th - 79	9th - 81	10th - 81
2nd Inns:	1st - 1	2nd - 1	3rd - 1	4th - 9	5th - 32	6th - 41	7th - 42	8th - 42	9th - 89	10th - 108

BONUS POINTS: SUSSEX 3, HAMPSHIRE 0 New Ball on completion of 100 overs.

Bowling Analysis	Ovs	Md	R	Wk	wd	nb	Ovs	Md	R	Wk	wd	nb
LEWRY	15.4	5	37	6	0	0	12.0	2	42	7	0	0
KIRTLEY	15.0	5	27	1	1	0	12.0	2	63	2	0	0
TAYLOR	10.0	8	5	2	0	2	0.2	0	1	1	0	0
DAVIS	2.0	0	5	0	0	0	0.0	0	0	0	0	0
ADAMS	2.0	0	6	1	0	0	0.0	0	0	0	0	0

RESULT: SUSSEX 18pts Won By An Innings & 113 Runs, HAMPSHIRE 3pts

UMPIRES

R. JULIAN
P. WILLEY

SCORERS

L.V. CHANDLER
V.H. ISAACS

Hours of Play

1st - 3rd Days - 11.00am - 6.30pm
4th Day - 11.00am - 6.00pm

LUNCH

1st - 3rd Days - 1.15pm - 1.55pm
4th Day - 1.00pm - 1.40pm

TEA

1st - 3rd Days - 4.10pm - 4.30pm or when 32 overs remain to be bowled, whichever is later
4th Day - 3.40pm - 4.00pm

Minimum Overs

1st, 2nd & 3rd Days - 104 overs
4th Day - 96 overs

1st Innings Bonus Points

awarded only for performances in the first 130 overs

Batting (Max 5pts)

1pt awarded on 200, 250, 300, 350 and 400 runs.

Bowling (Max 3pts)

1pt awarded on 3, 6 & 9 wickets

Match Points

Win 12pts & Draw 4pts plus 1st Inns Bonus Points

Sussex Score Updates

(01273) 827145

50p www.sussexcricket.co.uk

SUSSEX *v.* SOMERSET

19, 20 and 21 July 2002 County Championship
Taunton

It is surprising what a team can do, even when their captain and principal batsman and their vice-captain and leading bowler are absent. Chris Adams had suffered a calf strain and James Kirtley had been sidelined when, practising in the nets with the England one-day squad, he had broken a bone in his hand. Cometh the hour, cometh the man, so they say, and Richard Montgomerie stepped up to captain the team and promptly lost the toss to Somerset's Tasmanian, Jamie Cox.

Somerset's groundsman, Phil Frost, had provided an excellent pitch for the Friday morning, but the home side made poor use of it. In the first 39 overs, 7 wickets went down, as Billy Taylor, Jason Lewry and Kevin Innes knocked over the Somerset batsmen like ninepins. At 207 for 9, they looked as though they had missed the boat, but Matthew Bulbeck and Steffan Jones did better than any other pair and added 63 for the last wicket. Sussex could still be pleased with their work, especially when the established pair of Montgomerie and Murray Goodwin set off briskly and, although both of them were out by the time the score had reached 94, Tony Cottey, who was playing only because of the injury to Adams, ran to a 59-ball fifty and was well supported by Michael Yardy.

On the Saturday morning, a total of 500 seemed well within Sussex's grasp on this flattest of pitches. Tony Cottey ran to his second ton of the season with a six and 14 fours, and added 123 untroubled runs with Tim Ambrose before the events of the previous day threatened to repeat themselves. With Cottey and Ambrose gone and the Sussex middle-order failing, Somerset appeared to be clawing their way back into the game, as Sussex reached 351 for 7 wickets. The hosts, however, had not reckoned on Robin Martin-Jenkins and Mark Davis, who then batted through to the close, each making his highest score in

Mark Davis returns to the pavilion after scoring his maiden hundred for Sussex.

Frizzell County Championship - Division 1 Somerset v Sussex

Friday 19th - Monday 22nd July 2002

Umpires:- JH Evans, MJ Kitchen   Scorers:- G A Stickley, JF Hartridge

* = Captain
+= Wicket Keeper

Somerset won the toss & elected to Bat   Sussex won by an innings and 1 run

	SOMERSET	1st Innings		2nd Innings	
1.	J Cox (1) *	c Prior b Taylor	27	b Lewry	0
2.	MJ Wood (20)	c Prior b Taylor	31	c sub b Lewry	13
3.	M Burns (3)	c Taylor b Innes	26	c sub b Davis	98
4.	PD Bowler (13)	c Yardley b Innes	0	lbw b Lewry	20
5.	KA Parsons (6)	b Lewry	17	b Lewry	0
6.	ID Blackwell (15)	b Innes	18	c Ambrose b Taylor	114
7.	RJ Turner (5)+	lbw b Lewry	9	lbw b Taylor	31
8.	KP Dutch (17)	c Goodwin b Davis	30	c & b Davis	2
9.	PD Trego (21)	b Davis	26	b Taylor	4
10.	MPL Bulbeck (16)	not out	53	c Ambrose b Taylor	22
11.	PS Jones (11)	c Ambrose b Lewry	6	not out	37
12.	PCL Holloway (14)				

1st Innings: B. LB.5 W. 8 NB. 14 — EXTRAS: 27 — TOTAL: 270
2nd Innings: B.5 LB.13 W.6 NB.8 — EXTRAS: 32 — TOTAL: 373

BONUS POINTS: BATTING: 2   BOWLING:

RUNS AT FALL OF WICKET: 1-51 2-82 3-94 4-94 5-116 6-138 7-153 8-206 9-207
1-0 2-23 3-63 4-63 5-191 6-276 7-299 8-305 9-306

BOWLING ANALYSIS	O	M	R	W	O	M	R	W
JD Lewry	16.2	3	84	3	22	1	112	4
RSC Martin-Jenkins	20	2	67	0	14	3	43	0
BV Taylor	20	8	56	2	20.2	3	68	4
KJ Innes	4	0	28	3	13	4	44	0
MH Yardy	4	0	10	0				
MJG Davis	4	1	20	2	19	0	88	2

	SUSSEX	1st Innings		2nd Innings
1.	RR Montgomerie *	c Bowler b Trego	25	
2.	TR Ambrose	c Bowler b Parsons	68	
3.	JD Lewry	c Wood b Jones	0	
4.	MJ Goodwin	c Turner b Burns	42	
5.	MJ Prior	st Turner b Parsons	8	
6.	PA Cottey	c Trego b Parsons	120	
7.	RSC Martin-Jenkins	not out	205	
8.	MH Yardy	c Bowler b Blackwell	36	
9.	KJ Innes	c Turner b Trego	3	
10.	MJG Davis	c Bowler b Jones	111	
11.	BV Taylor	c Turner b Jones	1	
12.	MA Robinson			

1st Innings: B. LB. 11 W.2 NB. 12 — EXTRAS: 25 — TOTAL: 644
2nd Innings: B. LB. W. NB. — EXTRAS: — TOTAL:

BONUS POINTS: BATTING: BOWLING: 3

RUNS AT FALL OF WICKET: 1-60 2-94 3-287 4-288 5-308 6-330 7-351 8-642 9-644
1- 2- 3- 4- 5- 6- 7- 8- 9-

BOWLING ANALYSIS	O	M	R	W	O	M	R	W
MPL Bulbeck	13	1	66	0				
PS Jones	40.3	6	159	3				
M Burns	17	3	77	1				
KA Parsons	19	2	67	3				
PD Trego	17	1	110	2				
ID Blackwell	30	9	112	1				
KP Dutch	15	1	42	0				

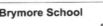

SCORING OF POINTS:

*For a win, 12 points plus points scored in 1st innings. *In a tie, each side scores 6 points plus points scored in 1st innings. *In a draw, each side score 4 points, plus points scored in 1st innings. *If scores are equal in drawn match, the side batting in 4th innings scores 6 points plus points scored in 1st innings. *1st innings points retained whatever the result of match.

BONUS POINTS:

Awarded in the first 130 overs of each first innings:

Batting:
- 200 to 249 runs = 1pt
- 250 to 299 runs = 2pts
- 300 to 349 runs = 3pts
- 350 to 399 runs = 4pts
- 400 plus = 5pts

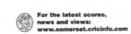

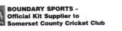

Bowling:
- 3 to 5 wkts. taken = 1pt
- 6 to 8 wkts. taken = 2pts
- 9 to 10 wkts. taken = 3pts

first-class cricket. By adding an unbroken 238, they eclipsed the previous Sussex eighth-wicket record made exactly one hundred years previously by Charles Smith and George Brann against Kent at Hove.

Sunday was not a day for quiet reflection for the Somerset side. Davis, who had been struck a painful blow on the hand by Jones when he had scored just 1 run (an injury later confirmed as a broken bone), soon reached his maiden hundred, while Martin-Jenkins, with a checked drive through extra cover, reached his double ton – a mighty leap forward from his previous highest score of 113. When Davis edged one to slip, the pair were just a run short of the English 8th-wicket record set in 1896 by Bobby Peel and Lord Hawke for Yorkshire against Warwickshire. When the Sussex innings closed on 644 – Montgomerie was enjoying his captaincy role and had no thoughts of a declaration – Martin-Jenkins was left on 205*, having faced 233 balls and struck a six and 29 fours. It was the County's highest total since their 670 for 9 declared against Northamptonshire at Hove in 1921.

After this feast of runs, the Sussex bowlers showed maximum commitment on a pitch that was still full of runs. Jason Lewry, the season's beneficiary, took the first four wickets and, although Michael Burns and Ian Blackwell batted well for Somerset, there was only ever going to be one result and the match ended with Sussex having an innings and just 1 run to spare.

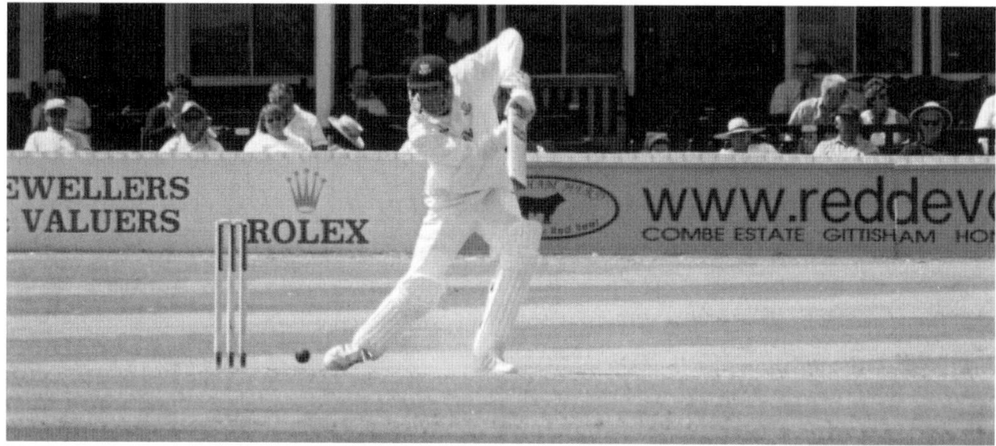

Robin Martin-Jenkins drives on the off-side to reach his double hundred.

Robin Martin-Jenkins and Mark Davis show off their magnificent partnership.